GUYS CAN BE CAT LADIES TOO

MICHAEL SHOWALTER

GUYS CAN BE
CAT LADIES TOO

ABRAMS IMAGE   NEW YORK

CONTENTS

Part Three: Advanced Cat
Your cat is your life.

Introduction

1. **"Girlfriend Has a Cat Guy"**
   You've just met the woman of your dreams, but she has a cat. You think cats are weird and aloof, but she's obsessed with the cat. You're afraid that if you can't get on board with the cat, she'll dump you.

2. **"Roommate Has a Cat Guy"**
   Your new roommate has a cat. You really like your roommate, and more important you really like your room, but the cat scares you and freaks you out and won't leave you alone, and now you're thinking about either killing it or moving out.

3. **"Boss Has a Cat Guy"**
   Your boss has cats. He wants to show you pictures of them all the time, but to you they just look like big, hairy squirrel faces, and you're afraid that if you don't act all gooey about it, you'll lose your job and become a hobo.

4. **"Moving In with Your Girlfriend Guy"**
   You and your main squeeze are finally moving in together, but you're worried that her cats won't like you and will treat you like you're some kind of creepy new boyfriend trying to edge in on their territory.

5. **"Cat-Curious Guy"**
   You're a guy and you just straight up want a cat, but you're afraid of these new feelings. "If I get a cat, will I ever get laid again?" you ask yourself. Admit it: You're cat curious.

Hello, future fellow Cat Lady Guy, and welcome to this book!

If any of these guys sound like you, then you've come to the right place. Let's face it: you, like so many other dudes, have zero idea how to deal with a cat. It's like they say, "Men are from Mars, cats are from Venus." Cats are as alien as, well, aliens.

Cats are complicated, and though you retain many endearing qualities (you can crush a beer can on your forehead, you can juggle a Hacky Sack and talk on the phone at the same time, you can recite entire South Park episodes by heart), you lack the refinement and sensitivities necessary for successful cat cohabitation.

And really, at the end of the day, don't you want to be more than just a "dude" who "lives with a cat"? Don't you seek a relationship beyond just "roomies"? Don't you want to *share your life with something*? And then, if it goes well, get another one? Maybe there are multiple cats that strike your fancy. Get five! Get twenty-five! No judgment here. One man's pepper is another man's porridge.

"But, Mike, I'm hopeless! I tried to pet my girlfriend's cat and it hissed at me and scratched my face."

Fret not, [insert your name], because in these pages, I will teach you and all other guys, even the most hopeless of Neanderthals, everything you need to know so that you can get along with, appreciate, understand, and, yes, love that most mysterious and elusive of God's creatures: the domestic house cat. Before too long, [insert your name], you'll be doing a lot more than just petting your cat, I promise you that.

Allow this guide to take you on a journey of self-discovery—in the span of 176 pages you will be transformed from a butt-picking, misshapen, semi-incompetent caveman into a true pet-loving gentleman, into maybe, just maybe, a *FULL. FLEDGED. CAT LADY.* That's right, you heard me correctly, a Cat Lady.

Fellas, if you complete my course all the way to its final chapter, you too can walk around all day in sweatpants mumbling to yourself about coupons while thousands of little cat eyes watch your every move. You too can share meaningful conversations that are one part "Here, kitty!" to two parts "Meow!"

Because you know what, friend?

Guys can be cat ladies too.

A Note to Girlfriends, Roommates, and Wives

First let me say that I understand you and what you've been through and what he's put you through and what he's put your cat or cats through and I want you to know that your guy is in good hands with me. He is unquestionably a hard case, pathetic even, but in my experience no situation is too difficult to overcome. It will take time, of course. We will need to break him down and rebuild from the first brick. He must unlearn what little he already knows and be taught new things. But I assure you, it can be done. My only advice is that you please try to be patient and supportive during this turbulent time as he learns how to become a more complete person.

GUY

SUPER
COOL HAIR

SLY SMIRK
OR GRIN

ARMS
GOOD FOR
CARRYING
THINGS +
DRIVING
A CAR

DEVIL-MAY-CARE
ATTITUDE

BIG
MUSCLES
FROM BEING
SO ATHLETIC

CAT

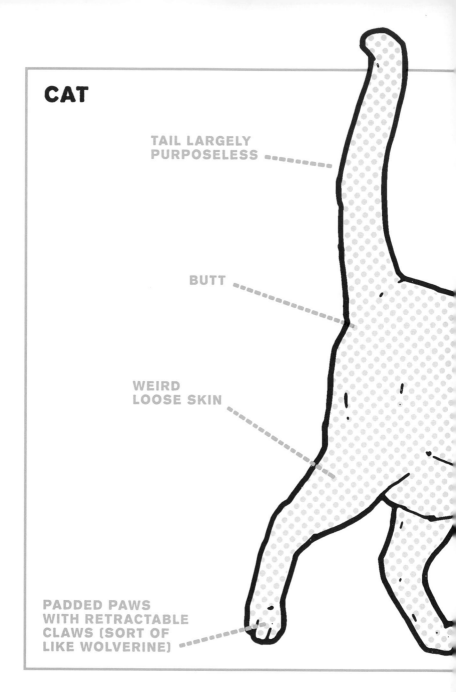

TAIL LARGELY
PURPOSELESS ------

BUTT ------

WEIRD
LOOSE SKIN ------

PADDED PAWS
WITH RETRACTABLE
CLAWS (SORT OF
LIKE WOLVERINE) ------

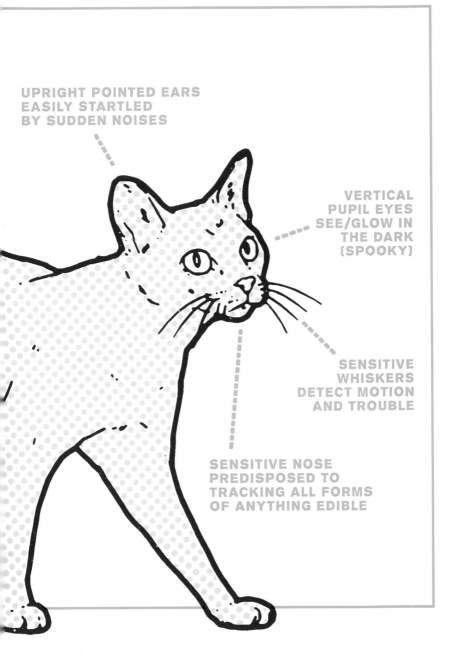

UPRIGHT POINTED EARS
EASILY STARTLED
BY SUDDEN NOISES

VERTICAL
PUPIL EYES
SEE/GLOW IN
THE DARK
(SPOOKY)

SENSITIVE
WHISKERS
DETECT MOTION
AND TROUBLE

SENSITIVE NOSE
PREDISPOSED TO
TRACKING ALL FORMS
OF ANYTHING EDIBLE

CAT LADY

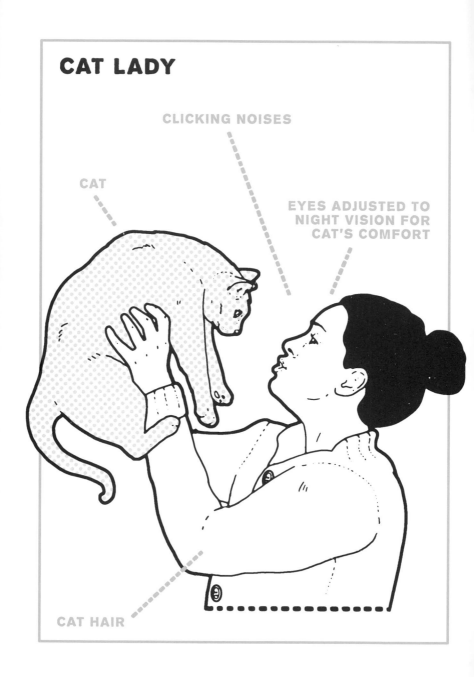

CLICKING NOISES

CAT

EYES ADJUSTED TO
NIGHT VISION FOR
CAT'S COMFORT

CAT HAIR

CAT LADY GUY

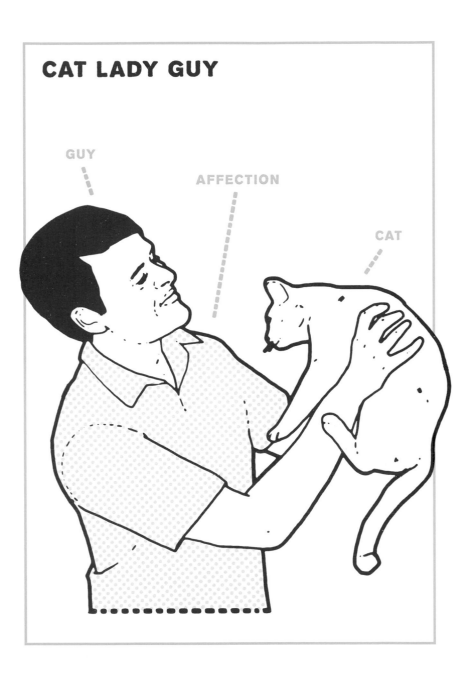

PART ONE

BEGINNER CAT

What is a cat? Sounds like a silly question, right? But for so many men, it is a legitimate query. We are conditioned from an early age not to ask questions, and for that we pay the price as ignorant, yet curious adults. This book removes the stigma and encourages you to ask away.

Let's start with the basics.

CHAPTER 1

What Is a Cat?

cat — *noun* \'kat\

a. a carnivorous mammal (*Felis catus*) long domesticated as a pet for catching rodents
b. companion of humans noted for its pointy ears, whiskers, and long catlike tail
c. a cool jazz musician known for being well dressed, good at playing a brass instrument, and also having a way with the ladies.

Have I got your attention now? Have you already learned something you didn't know before?

A BRIEF HISTORY OF CATS

Cats were first domesticated in the Neolithic period, but really came into popularity as prized pets in ancient Egypt, where they were worshipped as gods. Cats were also admired in ancient Rome and appreciated for their mice-hunting skills in the Far East.

The Middle Ages saw a dark time for cats, as the tide of public opinion turned toward "cats are the devil." The ill-informed masses massacred cats by the thousands, and the Western world paid a heavy price for its unwise War on Cats: the decrease in cat population led to an increase in rat population, and, ultimately, to the Black Death of 1348.

The Black Death is also referred to as "the Great Plague" and "the Great Pestilence."

It was a devastating outbreak of bubonic plague that hit Europe in 1348.

Bubonic plague is a zoonotic disease, which is an infectious disease transmitted between species.

Bubonic plague is transmitted from rats to fleas to humans.

The Renaissance ushered in an era of open-mindedness, where artistic skill and scientific thought flourished. This rebirth, unfortunately, meant more death for cats. Thought to aid "witches" (primitive cat ladies) with their "potions" (soups) and "spells" (crazy talk), cats were often burned at the stake and thrown from cliffs (bummer).

It wasn't until the 1800s that Western aristocrats rediscovered the true nature of the cat, which the ancient Egyptians, Mesopotamians, Chinese, Buddhists, Burmese, Siamese, and Japanese knew long before: cats are exquisite, endlessly fun to watch, and very cute! The advent of unique cat breeds and cat shows further elevated the cat to prestige status, and it soon became the rage again to keep a cat (or two or three or ten or twenty) in the home.

The cat truly received its due as inspiration for genius when a young Nikola Tesla first became fascinated with electricity when he petted his cat and received a shock. That's right! You can thank cats for the advent of lightbulbs! Cats were able to fulfill their patriotic duty during World War I, when the British army deployed five hundred thousand cats as gas detectors and ratters in the trenches, and during World War II when the U.S. Army's 13th Armored Division, aka the Black Cats, selected the fine feline as its mascot and namesake. Pretty cool, huh?

WHO WAS NIKOLA TESLA?

Tesla was a Serbian American inventor, engineer, and scientist whose discoveries led to the invention of the lightbulb.

Tesla worked for Thomas Edison early in his career; Edison is largely credited with inventing the lightbulb.

In 2005 Tesla was nominated for the "Greatest American" honor on the Discovery Channel; unfortunately, he died sixty-two years prior and was unable to attend the television event.

At some point the "dog is a man's best friend" maxim entered the general consciousness, and although a resurgence of cat love emerged in the twentieth century, cats continue to be stereotyped in the media as "lazy," "fat," and "evil." Cats have long been thought to boast nine lives, but this theory has yet to be proven. A competing theory is that many cats simply have one extremely *lucky* life.

"What do they eat?"

Cats are obligate carnivores, which means that meat must be the central component of their diet. Meat contains a high amount of protein, which is in turn composed of amino acids. The most important amino acid in a cat's diet is taurine.[1] Moisture is a second key component in the feline diet. Canned or pouched food must contain 60 to 80 percent water for a cat to be well hydrated. Cats will also eat mice and bugs, if allowed access to them. If you're still reading this paragraph I'm impressed.

"How many different types of cats are there?"

The International Progressive Cat Breeders' Alliance recognizes seventy-three breeds of cats. However, the Cat Fanciers' Association, a more conservative organization, recognizes a mere forty-one. That's a difference of twenty-eight cats!

"Why are cats so weird?"

People thought David Bowie was weird too. Does that answer your question?

"How come when I pick it up it meows and wriggles away?!"

Okay friend, let's not get ahead of ourselves. We'll get to that.

---

[1]   Taurine is also one of the main ingredients in Red Bull energy drinks and the reason snowboarding daredevil and pinup heartthrob Shaun White has such "catlike" reflexes.

CHAPTER 2

What Is *Not* a Cat?

Now that we know the basics of what is a cat, let's take it a step further and look at what is *not* a cat.

not a cat — *noun* \\'nät\\ \\'ā\\ \\'kat\\

a. anything that is not a cat
b. a dog, a person, a chair, a toaster strudel, a six-pack of beer, a football, a chimichanga—none of these things are cats
c. anything else that is not a cat

HOW CAN I BE SURE IT'S A CAT OR NOT A CAT?

It's perfectly natural to confuse cats for not-cats and not-cats for cats, particularly if you are new to cats, or really stupid. The easiest way to tell if something is a cat is to review this simple checklist:

1. Does it meow?
2. Does it have a tail?
3. Is it really cute?
4. Does it like hiding inside bags?
5. Is it a cat?

If you answered in the positive to any of the above, especially #5, then the thing in question is most likely a cat.

CHAPTER 3

What Are Some Other Things I Should Know?

Okay, let's check in. You've learned what a cat *is* and you've also learned what a cat *isn't*, but did you know there are *other* things you should know?

The following is literally a list of basic things that you should know.

- How to build a fire
- How to perform CPR
- How to make a sandwich
- How to make spaghetti
- How to change a tire
- How to swim and guide a canoe
- How to tie a knot
- How to identify different types of poisonous plants
- How to pick a lock

Remember: you have nothing to offer a cat if you have nothing to offer yourself. Becoming a Cat Lady Guy isn't just about becoming a Cat Lady Guy, it's about becoming an all-around better person.

So I encourage you to carefully study the following instructional pictorial diagrams and strongly advise *against* skipping this section altogether and proceeding straight to the cat stuff.

HOW TO PERFORM CPR*

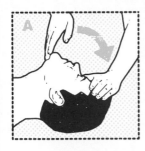

TOUCH THE CHIN AND FOREHEAD

PUSH ON THE CHEST

BLOW INTO THE OTHER PERSON'S MOUTH

HOW TO BUILD A FIRE*

ADD TINDER

STACK KINDLING

LIGHT BASE

(*ABRIDGED VERSIONS)

CHAPTER 4

Can Cats Do That?

Now that we are familiar with *what cats are*, in this next chapter, we will begin to learn about *what cats can do*.

CATS CAN EAT

EATING FACTS

Healthy, active adult cats require approximately 30 calories per pound of body weight a day.

For an average-size cat (around 8 pounds), this translates into approximately ⅓ cup of dry food or 6 ounces of wet food.

Do feed your cat twice a day—morning and night.

If you can't feel your cat's ribs, your cat is overweight.

Cats will eat anything and have terrible table manners.

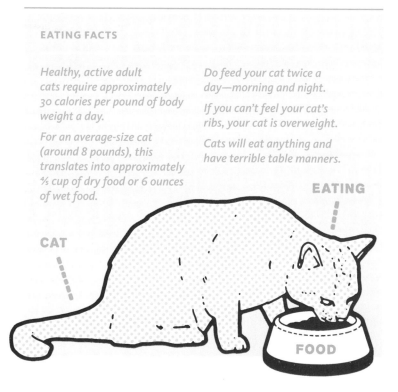

EATING

CAT

FOOD

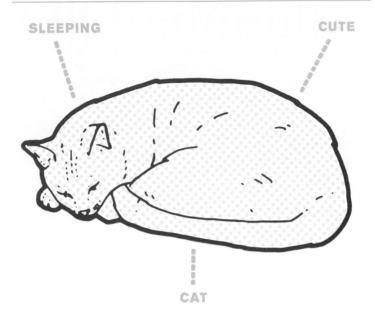

SLEEPING   CUTE

CAT

SLEEPING FACTS

Wild cats and domesticated cats will sleep from sixteen to twenty hours a day.

Cats are always on alert, even during sleep.

Cats are crepuscular, not nocturnal, meaning their activity peaks at dawn and dusk.

Cats are mind-bogglingly cute when they sleep. You will never tire of watching them take naps.

FUN FAKE CAT FACT: Did you know that the John Steinbeck novel *Of Mice and Men* was written by a cat?

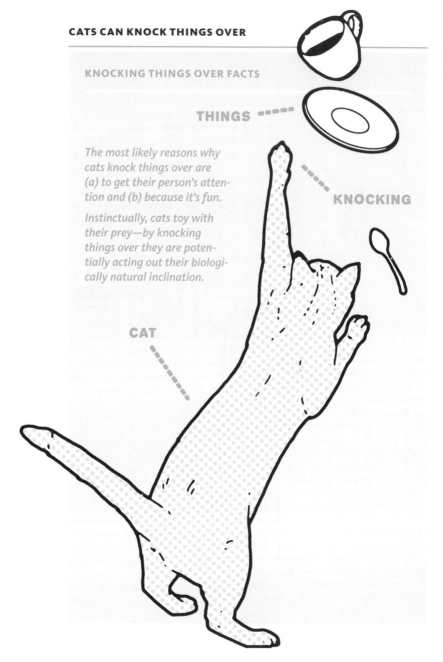

KNOCKING THINGS OVER FACTS

THINGS

KNOCKING

The most likely reasons why cats knock things over are (a) to get their person's attention and (b) because it's fun.

Instinctually, cats toy with their prey—by knocking things over they are potentially acting out their biologically natural inclination.

CAT

CATS CAN CLIMB INTO BAGS

CLIMBING INTO BAG FACTS

Cats like feeling cozy and secure, and small spaces (such as bags) offer this snug sense of enclosure.

Cats derive security from believing that no one can see them.

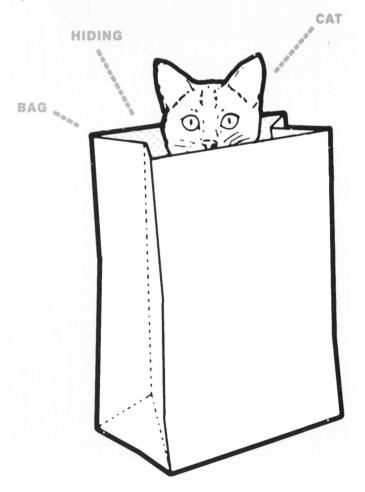

CAT

HIDING

BAG

These are the primary things that cats can do, but not the only things they can do. Here's a list of secondary cat behaviors.

- Cats can scratch furniture
- Cats can stretch
- Cats can sit on the computer while you work
- Cats can reject food
- Cats can bathe in the sun
- Cats can hide in drawers
- Cats can jump up onto the top of your refrigerator
- Cats can stare through you as if you're not even there

THE "DOG PROBLEM"

I've just named twelve amazing things that cats can do, but you're still on the fence. You're thinking: "Sure, cats are great but . . ."

"*. . . My dog plays and can tell when I have low blood sugar!*"

"*. . . My dog helps blind people!*"

"*. . . My dog saves mountain climbers!*"

"*. . . My dog solves murders!*"

All of these things are true. And guess what? There's a bunch more things that dogs can do that cats can't do. Dogs can swim. Dogs can take cash out of an ATM. I've seen dogs buy groceries and carry them home. The dog in that French movie almost won an acting award! But here's the thing: it's not a competition. We can love dogs *and* cats! Isn't that a crazy idea?

Can you imagine what the world would be like if we created baseless competitions everywhere?

"Spoons are better than forks! Get rid of all forks!"

Why do that? Spoons are great and forks are too.

"Pants are more versatile than sweaters!"

Isn't there room enough in this world for pants *and* sweaters?

"I love soup! Abolish salad!"

What? Why?! What about soup *and* salad? Many restaurants and buffets offer *both*.

Do you see my point? It's not a competition.

By loving cats you are not dissing dogs. There should be room enough for dogs *and* cats in your life.

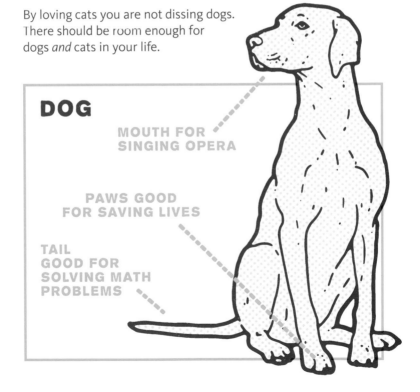

DOG

MOUTH FOR
SINGING OPERA

PAWS GOOD
FOR SAVING LIVES

TAIL
GOOD FOR
SOLVING MATH
PROBLEMS

CHAPTER 5

Why Is It So Cute When They Stick Their Tongues Out Like This?

Just a fact of life, I guess.

CHAPTER 6

How Will I Know When I'm Ready for a Cat?

This is the question I most frequently encounter. Guys from every walk of life approach me and say, "Mike, I want to take that next step in my life and get a cat, but how do I know when I ready?"

Guys, here's the thing: the most important relationship you'll ever have in your life is the one you have with yourself. Surprised I said that, huh? But it's true. How you feel about and care for your own mind, body, and spirit sets the stage for all relationships outside yourself—*specifically* with your cat. Think about it: if you don't love yourself, then how can you love a cat?

Here are some signs that you are ready to love yourself enough to allow a cat into your life. Think of these not as things you must have, but rather as aspirations along your journey toward becoming a Cat Lady Guy.

You complete yourself. You don't need a cat to feel whole. You are a capable, independent individual, and a cat in your life would simply be the frosting on the cake to make your life that much sweeter. If you can say, "I am okay without a cat," then you are ready for a cat!

You want a cat, but you don't need a cat. Remember item one? You complete yourself, and you don't *need* a cat to make you *you*. Sure, a cat will make you so much better than you already are in so many ways it's impossible to list them all, but let's not get ahead of ourselves. You *want* a better life, but you don't *need* it.

You smile every day. You're no longer a brooding, self-absorbed, Camus-reading drag who whines, "What can I get?" Rather, you look deep within yourself and ask the universe, "What can I *give*?" You're happy! You can't help yourself! Your joy is contagious.

You're willing to take risks. You will know you're ready when you're not asking "Am I ready?" You'll just dive in and pick a cat.

You build memories, not barriers. Your cat cannot be a compartmentalized portion of your life, accessed by you only when convenient. You must be willing to create a life *together* with your cat. Let your cat lead the way to a whole new level of being.

WHAT WE'VE LEARNED

- Cats are carnivorous mammals long domesticated as pets for catching rodents.

- Cats are not dogs, chairs, or six-packs of beer.

- You can be a cat lady too, if you put your mind to it.

  Use the blank area opposite to "riff" free-associatively on anything else you've learned.

EXERCISE 1 What Else I've Learned
by _____ [your name]

*Free-write in the blank space below about what it means to be a
cat caretaker. Be honest. You may be surprised by what you write.*

I've learned . . .

I've learned . . .

I've learned . . .

I've learned . . .

I've learned . . .

I've learned . . .

EXERCISE 2 Identifying Types

*Go into a crowded public space and see if you can tell the differ-
ence between the cats, the guys, the ladies, the cat ladies, and
the cat lady guys. Write everything down in a journal and keep
track of your findings.*

GAMES + PUZZLES

EASY SUDOKU

5	8	6	3	7	4	9	1	2
1	3	7	9	5	2	8	6	4
2	4	9	8	1	6	5	7	3
8	7	2	5	4	3	1	9	6
6	9	3	7		1	2	4	5
4	1	5	6	2	9	7	3	8
9	5	4	2	3	7	6	8	1
7	2	1	4	6	8	3	5	9
3	6	8	1	9	5	4	2	7

BRAIN TEASER

Q: *If one cat leaves Chicago running 100 mph and a different cat leaves New York City traveling 150 mph and the distance between the two cites is 600 miles, how far from New York will the cats be when they pass each other?*

A: *It's a trick question because the cat from Chicago decided to take a nap in Pittsburgh and screwed the whole thing up.*

CONNECT THE DOTS

Conect any dot from the left side with any dot on the right side and see what the spaghetti looks like after the cat knocked it over.

FIND ALL THE WORDS RELATED TO CATS AND GUYS

```
B B A L L S O F S T R I N G T E B C
A A C R F O G H W S Q T R L V R O A
R A D P A D P T Q H W A N R O B O T
B L W G M A O C M I L K A L X X B S
E O I F K E B R O R A I A S A S S Y
C A N S O F O O D T A N A X S O U P
U X D I M O B A R F U G A L P U R R
E I S P Y A F F I N G N A P O K R A
S O U P T G B O N G W A T E R B L C
V A R B U C E T K X X P A K T B M T
W A F O R B E R S T M S B U S W P I
W H I S K E R S T I P O P M U S I C
Y A N I E B C Y U G I F E M E W B E
R U G B Y B A G F O O T B A L L E W
C A Q P W G N X F E B E H Y C P E W
T U N A F I S H X H A N G I N O U T
```

Balls of string, cats, practice (you know, like for a sport), hangin' out, tuna fish, rugby, whiskers, pop music, taking naps often, robot, soda, cans o' food, barbecues, barf, bongwater, sports, okra, turkey, beer cans, windsurfing, T-shirt, milk, drink stuff, purr, bro, tan, rad, pad. (Extra credit: Try to guess which are cat words, which are guy words, and which are both.)

BRAIN TEASER

Q: My cat regularly knocks the vase off of our kitchen counter. The vase costs 30 dollars. How many vases does the cat need to knock over before I stop buying vases?

A: Only you can answer that question. I will say, though, that the cat probably won't stop knocking the vases over, so if you're thinking you can convince him otherwise, you're mistaken.

CAT LADY PROGRESS REPORT #1:
CAN YOU CORRECTLY IDENTIFY THE CAT?

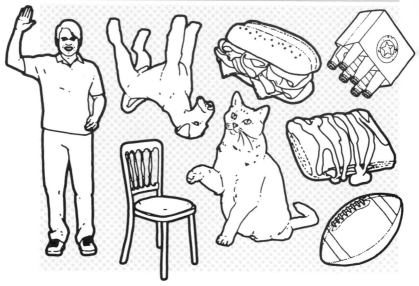

BE VERY CAREFUL, IT'S VERY DIFFICULT!

If you found the cat, *good job*! The next step is to find you a real-life cat and make you a cat person.

It takes a special type of individual to assume complete and total responsibility for a cat—it's not for everyone. But once you've learned the basics of cat rearing and raising, you will find that you actually *like* your new status as caretaker. You will begin to feel a sense of purpose—this cat can't function without you! You are needed! And you will begin to see *elements of yourself* in your cat. Sick satisfaction? Narcissistic self-expression? Perhaps. But once you're a cat person you won't care what other (jealous) people say.

Please ready yourself with an arsenal of tuna, Claritin, empty bags, and love!

CAT FOOD PYRAMID

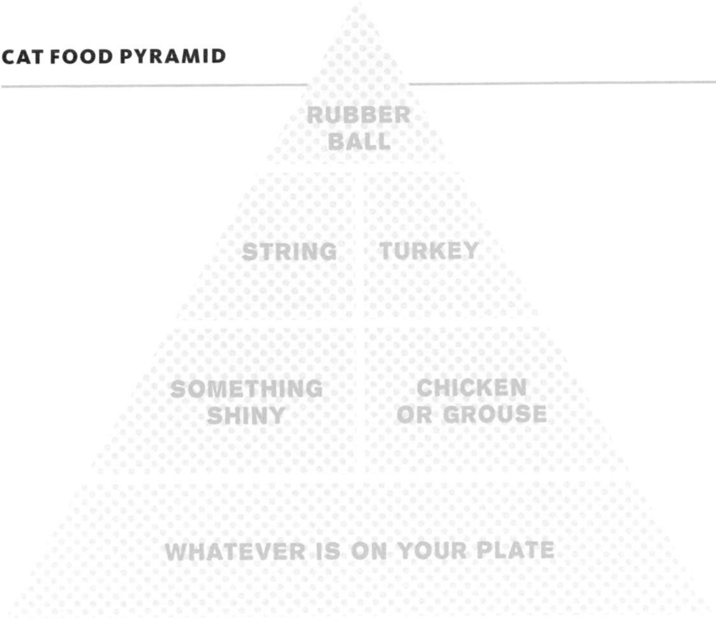

RUBBER
BALL

STRING   TURKEY

SOMETHING   CHICKEN
SHINY   OR GROUSE

WHATEVER IS ON YOUR PLATE

FACT OR FICTION?

Cats love milk.
FACT!
But . . . it gives them diarrhea. Scientists postulate that cats do
not love diarrhea.

Cats can see in the dark.
FACT!
That's why they don't need night-vision goggles.

Cats hate dogs.
FICTION!
Google "cat + dog + video" and you will see what I mean.

ASK MIKE!

YOU ASKED, I ANSWERED

"Why does my girlfriend's cat act all aloof like that?"

Clearly your girlfriend's cat has other things going on right now. Take a breather and check back later.

"How come my roommate's cat hisses at me when I poke it?"

Probably because you're poking it. I'd suggest you stop poking it.

"Do cats like pizza as much as I do?"

No, sadly, they do not. Cats like that *you* like pizza, and you are more than welcome to continue eating it, by all means. But it's not really their thing. And, to be fair, you *really* like pizza. You'd be hard-pressed to find anyone who likes pizza as much as you do.

"Should I teach my cat Spanish?"

It certainly can't hurt. Anything can help your cat get a leg up in the competitive job market.

"Do cats really have nine lives?"

Theoretically yes, but *do not attempt to test this theory at home. The results could be tragic.*

"This cat's poop smells funny. Should I keep smelling it?"

Nah, I'd say you've had enough for one day, bud.

"Sometimes my roommate's cat glares at me in such a way that it seems as though it's plotting my demise. Is this true?"

Possibly. Did you do anything to offend it? Remember that cats have very real feelings, and those feelings can be hurt just like yours and mine.

"I know cats kill mice, but can they fight crime?"

They can, but they are undercover cat cops and if I reveal any additional information it'll blow their cover.

"Do cats laugh?"

They laugh on the inside.

"Do chicks dig cologne?"

Depends on the chick, depends on the cologne. My tentative answer is "Sooooometimes?"

DID YOU KNOW . . . ?

- Cats have thirty-two muscles in each ear.
- Cats hate the smell of lemons.
- Egyptians shaved their eyebrows as a sign of mourning when their cats died.
- In English, cat is *cat*. In French, cat is *chat*. In German, cat is *Katze*. In Spanish, cat is *gato*. In Italian, cat is *gatto*. In Japanese, cat is *neko*. In Arabic, cat is *kitte*.
- Cats are partially color-blind.

VENN DIAGRAM: GUYS + CAT LADIES

Not all guys are cat ladies, and not all cat ladies are guys. But many people are both.

GUYS	BOTH	CAT LADIES
LEAVE TOILET SEAT UP	SPEAK MORE WITH CAT(S) THAN PARENTS	ALWAYS USE TOILET SEAT COVERS, EVEN IN OWN HOME
CAN (AND WILL) SUBSIST SOLELY ON CEREAL	ARE INCAPAPBLE OF MAKING PERSONAL PLANS WITHOUT CONSULTING CAT(S) AND OBTAINING TACIT APPROVAL	CAN (AND WILL) SUBSIST SOLELY ON LEAN CUISINES
ACT ON LOGIC (AND ALSO EMOTION)	ARE LIABLE TO CANCEL PLANS IF SENSING CAT'(S) DISAPPROVAL	ACT ON EMOTION (LOGICALLY DETERMINED EMOTION)

These are all tremendous books, and I urge you to read them, but at the very least buy them and keep them around your apartment for visitors and health inspectors to notice and appreciate:

Chicken Soup for the Soul: I Can't Believe My Cat Did That!: 101 Stories about the Crazy Antics of Our Feline Friends, by Jack Canfield, Mark Victor Hansen, and Jennifer Quasha

Cat Miracles: Inspirational True Stories of Remarkable Felines, by Brad Steiger and Sherry Hansen Steiger

Herding Cats: A Life in Politics, by Trent Lott

Crafting with Cat Hair: Cute Handicrafts to Make with Your Cat, by Kaori Tsutaya

Dewey: The Small-Town Library Cat Who Touched the World, by Vicki Myron, with Bret Witter

Julia's Cats: Julia Child's Life in the Company of Cats, by Patricia Barey and Therese Burson

What Is My Cat Thinking?: The Essential Guide to Understanding Pet Behavior, by Gwen Bailey

I Will See You in Heaven (Cat Lover's Edition), by Jack Wintz

Angel Cats: Divine Messengers of Comfort, by Allen Anderson and Linda Anderson

The Aristocats (novelization of the Disney movie)

Cats love music, and you love music about, for, and by cats. Stock up on these classic albums. They make intriguing napping spots for cats, and once they scratch them enough the records will skip, alleviating the need to get up and change the album.

Cat Stevens Complete: Songs from 1970–1975, by Yusuf Islam

Cats: Complete Original Broadway Cast Recording, by Andrew Lloyd Webber

Music Cats Love: While You Are Gone, by Bradley Joseph (including the hits "Paws and Claws," "Purrfect Mood," "Window Watching," and "A Sunny Spot")

Everybody Wants to Be a Cat: Disney Jazz, Vol. 1, by Roy Hargrove

Here Comes Santa Claws, by the Jingle Cats

Stray Cats Greatest Hits, by the Stray Cats

Cat Scratch Fever, by Ted Nugent

Mood Music for Cats (and Cat Lovers): A Ball of Twine, by Cheryl Christine

Cool for Cats, by Squeeze

The Truth about Cats and Dogs: Original Motion Picture Soundtrack, by Howard Shore

PART TWO

INTERMEDIATE CAT

You did it! You're ready! You know what a cat is. You know what a cat *isn't*. You know what a cat can do. You know what it *can't* do. You know how to tie a knot, build a fire, and identify different types of poisonous plants. You're ready, both functionally and emotionally, for a cat. You're becoming a man and I'm proud of you. If I were with you right now I'd be giving you a serious "cat fist bump."

Fella, you're ready to find that special cat-someone. It's time to make a match!

CHAPTER 7

Choosing Your Ideal Cat Mate

A lot of guys think that choosing a cat is as easy as sticking their hand into a box of kittens and hoping for the best. *This could not be further from the truth*. It's actually more difficult to find a good cat mate than a human soul mate. Why? Because when humans first meet, they are able to use language to exchange basic, vital information like "I'm an outdoorsy gal" or "I'm not so much into spy movies" or "I suffer from night terrors." This information helps determine compatibility. When it comes to choosing a cat, you'll need to make an educated guess. So let's get you educated.

WHO AM I?

The more we know about *you*, the more we can determine which type of cat will offer the best chance for successful cohabitation and fulfilling companionship.

What follows is a questionnaire that our in-house experts have created to match your personality type with the perfect cat. Please take your time and answer *honestly*. We need to know who you are, not whom you wish you could be.

MEET OUR EXPERTS

DR. JEFF SCHMERTMER, CLINICAL PSYCHOLOGIST
MANITOBA INSTITUTE OF CLINICAL PSYCHOLOGY

DR. NANCY FERMTERFER, PSYCHOTHERAPIST
CALGARY INSTITUTE OF PSYCHOTHERAPY

Your friends describe you as . . .

a. High maintenance—you constantly need your ego stroked.
b. Medium maintenance—you are fully able to entertain yourself, but you'll likely create a mess.
c. Low maintenance—eat, sleep, eat, sleep . . . what more could you need out of life?
d. Computer maintenance—so long as the PC you built yourself is humming, you're A-OK.
e. "High" maintenance—you're you, but you're high on pot. Get it? "High" maintenance.
f. Totally not mainstream maintenance—like, whatever, mon.

Your ideal home boasts . . .

a. Marble, stainless steel, and a Japanese super toilet.
b. A 72-inch plasma big-screen TV and an ESPN RedZone subscription.
c. Cacti and sacred incense.
d. The entire Criterion Collection on Blu-ray and more PlayStation games than you can shake a light saber at (but don't actually shake the light saber—it's in its original packaging).
e. A bong full of pot and the Cartoon Network.
f. This ratty old sofa? Classic flea market find. This macaroni art? Homemade, brother.

Your parents tease you for your . . .

a. Standing weekly appointment with Zac Efron's facialist.
b. That time you got arrested for streaking on Christmas Eve.
c. Your collection of exotic tree bark.
d. Lack of Internet.
d. "Toys"—but they're not toys, they're collectible novelty figurines, obviously.
e. Early-onset memory loss.
f. Intentionally poor personal hygiene.

Who is your celebrity man-crush?

a. Ryan Seacrest
b. Blake Griffin
c. Grizzly Adams
d. Wil Wheaton
e. Tommy Chong
f. Terry Richardson

Currently on your Kindle:

a. *Act Like a Lady, Think Like a Man*—better get one step ahead of the ladies.
b. *Freakonomics*—shit's freaky, dog!
c. . . . Kindle? Do you mean kindling for your fire?
d. *A Game of Thrones* (A Song of Ice and Fire #1)—it's a reread.
e. *Netflix for Dummies*.
f. Anything by Michael Chabon (even though you're not really reading it).

MOSTLY As

YOU ARE MANSOME AND YOU NEED A PERSIAN

You are gifted with impeccable taste and moderate to good interpersonal skills, but let's face it: you're a little vain. It is imperative that you be the center of attention in most every social situation (unless it bores you, in which case, ciao, hombres).

Persians are quiet, docile cats who require constant praise and daily grooming.

MOSTLY Bs

YOU ARE A BRO AND YOU NEED A MAINE COON

WHO WANTS TO PAAAARTTTY????

i LIKE SLEEPING ON WARM THINGS LIKE SWEATERS AND LAPTOPS.

You're one of the dudes, dude! You love sports, you love "kickin' it," "chillaxing," "keepin' it real," and so on. Toss you a brewski and you're good to go-skee.

Maine coons, like you, are friendly and "doglike." Big-boned, barrel-chested, outgoing—you two could be twins!

MOSTLY Cs

YOU ARE A MOUNTAIN MAN AND YOU NEED AN AMERICAN SHORTHAIR

You are equally as content meditating on a sunny rock as you are backpacking across Patagonia. Books are your friends, as are tea and Dr. Bronner's Magic All-One Soap.

American shorthairs are equally as content rubbing against your leg as they are sequestering themselves in a closet or staring at the side of the couch for hours. Gentle, curious, and blessed with longevity—get ready to have this guy around for twenty years at least!

MOSTLY Ds

YOU ARE A MAN CHILD AND YOU NEED AN ABYSSINIAN

TA DA!

MEOW.

You are a grown man, but you possess a childlike fascination with toys, games, and other sports of whimsy (read: more games). Nothing pleases you more than a PB+J prepared lovingly by your wife and/or mom.

Abyssinians are super friendly, love to play, and don't really mind when you feed them. They're perfect for kids—ergo, perfect for you.

MOSTLY Es

YOU ARE A POTHEAD AND YOU NEED A RAGDOLL

You're just keeping it mellow, man. That a crime now too?

Ragdolls *are laid-back, sweet, and big fans of lazing around. And like you, they're noted for their enthusiasm for food.*

MOSTLY Fs

YOU ARE A HIPSTER AND YOU NEED A FERAL CAT

WANNA START A BAND?

YEAH TOTALLY. I'LL PLAY GUITAR.

You were doing it (whatever "it" is) before it was cool (whenever that was, not like you're keeping track or nothing).

Feral cats are super nonconformist, so you guys should really hit it off.

Some of you may be thinking, "How bad could it really be if I have a cat that's not perfect for me? Cats are cats." Well, let me disabuse you of that notion, brother.

I got my first cat when I was twenty-three, fresh out of college, and certain that I knew everything about the world. I picked Mr. Bradley to be my cat not because I thought we were right for each other, but because I was naïve and arrogant enough to think that I was right for anyone.

We spent a year together, a year we both regretted. I wanted Mr. Bradley to be something he couldn't be. He wanted me to be man enough to meet him halfway in the relationship. Both of us were disappointed. I lost count of the nights wasted on the couch, me flipping channels, him pretending to sleep, until I'd feign a yawn, announce I was "tired," and sneak off to the bedroom to be alone with my loneliness.

After Mr. Bradley started pooping outside his litter box, we both knew there was no going back. I found an older couple that wanted a cat, and they took in Mr. Bradley, a cat that wanted more than I could give. To this day, I wonder what more I could have done. I ain't perfect, Jack, but I'm a better man now for what I went through then.

Once you know what you need, head to your nearest animal rescue and find your match. The hard part is over. The fun is about to begin.

CHAPTER 8

So You Have a Cat . . . Now What?

Okay, so you got yourself a cat (nice!) and you and your cat now share one roof. Shacking up with a cat takes a great deal of time, resources, and energy but you've done the "superficial relationship" thing and you're ready to get real now. Here's the deal: it's one thing to see a cat casually, but to actually cohabitate is a *much* bigger commitment. Trust me, it's worth it, but there are certain things you must learn.

THE CRUCIAL FIRST DAY

The first twenty-four hours of your new living arrangement will go a long way toward defining your relationship with your new cat. It's important to "set the tone" around the house, make her feel at home, clue her in to what's expected of her, and find out what she will need from *you* during this often turbulent transition period.

After the bags have been unpacked, the food and water inspected, and the litter box christened,[2] sit your cat down and have a casual, friendly conversation. I'm not asking you to give a

---

2   To christen your litter box, you must grab a handful of kitty litter and say, "Oh wah ta goo siam!" ten times fast.

big locker room speech. Frankly, it doesn't matter *what* you and your cat talk about. All that matters is that you open up those lines of communication right off the bat.

Here are five great conversation starters you and your cat might want to try:

1. *"So what's it like being a cat?"*

2. *"I'll tell you two things that are* true *about me and one that is untrue and you have to guess which one the* untrue *one is."*

3. *"This concussion issue is really going to be a problem for the NFL, huh?"*

4. *"Would you rather be rich and ugly or poor and attractive?"*

Now, I know what you're thinking right now and you're right. I said *five* conversation starters but only listed *four*. That's because I've left the fifth conversation starter open for you to fill in on your own.

5. [*What conversation starter would you like to suggest?*]

Here are some suggestions:

Do you believe in God?

What's your favorite TV show?

Do you enjoy travel?

Are you double jointed?

DO WEAR   DON'T WEAR

WHAT TO WEAR

It's important to dress for comfort for this first meeting, both to keep yourself relaxed and also to let the cat know that your house has a "chill vibe." A pair of well-worn jeans and a soft sweatshirt in a neutral color (beige, gray, or ecru) should do the trick.

WHAT NOT TO WEAR

Avoid clothes that have images of other animals on it. Remember, your cat has *no context* yet for this new world she has been dropped into. The last thing you want is for your cat to think she's also living with, say, a pack of wolves or a whole bunch of other cats she hasn't even met yet.

WHAT TO DO IF THE CAT THROWS UP ON YOU

If your cat throws up on you while you guys are talking, try not to make a big deal out of it. She might be nervous, and calling attention to the vomit on your jeans will only make her more anxious. Casually scoop up the mess and say something offhanded like "Hey, I do that all the time, cool that you do too." Many cats vomit as often as once a week, and it is rarely cause for concern.[3]

"MY CAT FELL ASLEEP WHILE I WAS TALKING TO HIM"

Welcome to the club, brother! Sleeping is the cat's "bread and butter," it's the cat's "jam," so to speak, so get used to it. The fact that your cat felt safe enough to drift into unconsciousness on the first day is actually a *great* sign. He's already feeling at home!

> **FUN CAT FACT:** Cats sleep up to 70 percent of the day. That means that if they live for ten years, they will have been fast asleep for seven of them.

---

3   Though it may also be a sign of intestinal worms, giardia, heat stroke, ulcers, hyperthyroidism, intestinal lymphoma, liver disease, renal failure, ruptured bladder, diabetes, or eating too fast. But other than that, it's not a cause for concern.

CHAPTER 9

What's In a Name?

Naming the new cat in your life can be overwhelming. What you name your cat says everything about you, everything about your cat, and everything about your life together. Show the world that you are a committed team with similar interests, and allow your cat's name to reflect that. Below is a guide to help you choose the perfect name based on your own interests.

IF YOU'RE A *FOODIE*

- Potato Chips
- Beef Wellington of Brussels Sprouts
- Gastrique
- Cloche
- Tartare

IF YOU'RE A *MOVIE BUFF*

- Bilbo Meow'gins
- Meow Vader
- Jason B'meow'ourne
- Cat Woman

IF YOU'RE *BUFF*

- Six-Pack
- Gainer Fuel
- Reps

IF YOU'RE A *WORDSMITH*

- Pelage
- Mellifluous
- Panacea

IF YOU'RE A *BLACKSMITH*

- Forging Heat

IF YOUR CAT'S A *PERSON*

- Jim
- Jeff
- Susan
- Andrew (Andy for short, but he hates it)

IF YOUR CAT'S A *PERSON, SUPER HIP EDITION*

- Imogen
- Juniper
- Tallulah
- Darwin

CHAPTER 10

Getting Your Cat Fixed

Cats are cute, we can all agree. But the last thing this world needs is a feline surplus—there are already plenty of amazing cats at your local shelter and roaming the streets that need a good home. So do the responsible thing, and bring your cat to the local vet to be spayed or neutered.

WHAT IS "SPAYING"?

"Spaying" is when you sterilize a female cat by surgically removing her ovaries and uterus.

WHAT IS "NEUTERING"?

"Neutering" is when you sterilize a male cat by surgically removing his testicles. Yup.

DOES IT HURT?

A properly licensed veterinarian should take all precautions to make sure your animal is sedated and kept comfortable while its sex organs are being removed. There will definitely be some soreness during recovery, and perhaps some psychological hurdles for your animal (though it doesn't know what happened, it may sense that something is missing/it is no longer "whole").

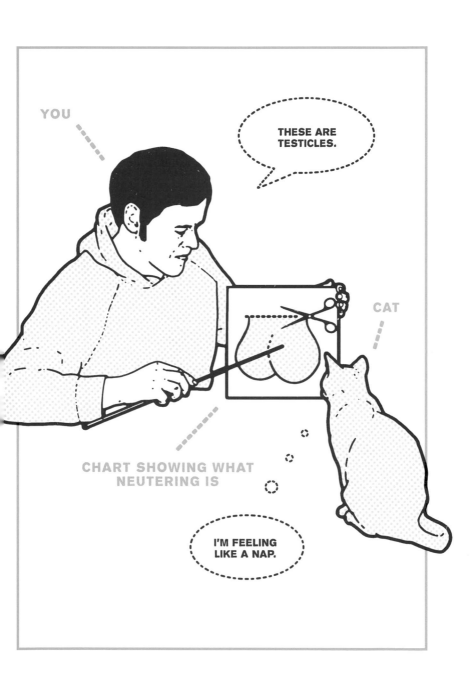

FINDING A VETERINARIAN

If you don't know where the closest vet is, use Google: enter the name of the town you live in, the word "vet," and the word "address." Pick one and schedule an appointment. You should be able to get one within one or two weeks unless the vet is extremely popular. (When vets are popular it means people like their work, so take that into account when choosing and scheduling.) Print out the driving directions and tape them to the dashboard of your car for easy viewing. Put your cat in the car, and drive to the address indicated.

PRE-OP: PREPARING YOUR CAT

Sit your cat down and explain what exactly the vet is going to do to him or her and why. (Example: "We're going to have your testicles/your uterus removed because we don't trust you with them/it.") If your cat seems confused (most won't have had a surgical procedure before), use the diagram on page 65 to help him or her understand what's about to happen.

POST-OP: HOW YOU CAN HELP

Though the procedure will be old hat for the vet, this will be a unique and likely difficult experience for your cat. Here are some tips for helping your guy or gal recuperate after the surgery.

- Provide your cat with a private area to rest and regroup in.

- Urge your cat not to be too active for the first few days—no running or jumping or knocking things over just yet.

- Use an Elizabethan collar to keep your cat from licking the wound.

- Rent some "feel-good" movies for you and your cat (e.g., *Mr. Holland's Opus* or *The Karate Kid*).

CHAPTER 11

How to Pet Your Cat

You've chosen your cat, you've named your cat, and you've removed its reproductive organs. Now let's learn how to pet your cat.

THE SNIFFER

THE APPETIZER

First, let the cat sniff your hand. This is both a means of introducing or reacquainting yourself with the cat and a warning that she is about to be petted.

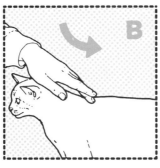

THE SWOOPER-DOOPER

THE MAIN COURSE

Second, *gently* swoop your hand along the top of the cat's head, and glide your hand backward. *Gently* is the key word. If it is helpful to mimic the motion of spreading butter or jelly on a piece of toast with your fingers, think of that.

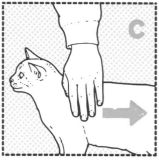

THE SWOOPER-DOOPER
PT. 2

WAY TO GO, MAN! KEEP DOING IT!

Third, repeat swoop-and-glide until you or the cat tires of the interaction. If the cat stretches its head into your hand, you are doing something right. Purring is also a good sign. Biting, scratching, swatting, and hissing most likely indicate that you're irritating the cat in some way and that you should probably stop and simply walk away.

THE NO-NO

NEVER PET "AGAINST THE GRAIN"

Cat fur naturally lays from the head toward the anus, and by petting in that direction you are helping to smooth your pet's coat and remove dead fur. You may be tempted to pet your cat from back to front, or "against the grain," but your cat will find this uncomfortable and will probably hiss at you and leave the room. Don't try to reinvent the wheel. There may be more than one way to *skin* a cat, but when it comes to petting, you've got only one option.

HOW TO SCRATCH YOUR CAT'S BELLY

First, approach your cat without startling her and crouch or kneel beside her. (Do not make direct eye contact. This is considered confrontational. Instead, hold your face at a three-quarters angle away from the cat's gaze.)

Second, make sure your cat knows you're about to scratch her belly. You may want to verbally express this to her. (Examples: "I'm about to scratch your belly"; "Get ready for a belly scratch"; "It's time to scratch your belly.")

Third, with two, three, four, or even five fingers, gently scratch your cat's belly as if you were sifting through a box of old record albums at a yard sale.

HOW TO PICK UP AND HOLD YOUR CAT

First, pet your cat's head several times as a way of saying, "Hi there, friend, get ready because I'm about to pick you up."

Second, as your hand completes its second or third swoop-and-glide motion, gently move your dominant hand underneath the cat, thus creating a bench or sofa effect with your forearm.

Third, use your body strength to lift the cat upward. In order to avoid injury, be sure to lift from your core and your legs rather than just your lower back.

Fourth, bring your cat close to your chest and repeat the petting motion on its head.

HOW TO PERFORM CAT BODY MASSAGE

Cats love massages. After a long, stressful day of lying around doing nothing, nothing's better than an attentive massage to help relax the body and get your cat ready for a good night's sleep. There are several different types of cat body massage:

Swedish massage utilizes classic European techniques to relieve tension and soothe tired muscles. There are five basic strokes. Long flowing strokes (*effleurage*) warm up the tissue. Kneading strokes (*petrissage*) encourage blood flow. Chopping strokes (*tapotement*) invigorate the muscles. Site-specific strokes (*friction*) work out tiny knots. And finally, shaking the muscles (*vibration*) stimulates the nerve endings.

> **FUN FACT ABOUT SWEDEN:** A couple of Swedish dudes, Carl Munters and Baltzar von Platen, invented the refrigerator with moving parts.

SWEDISH CAT MASSAGE

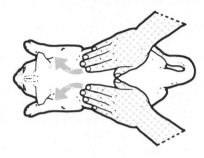

EFFLEURAGE

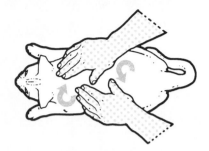

PETRISSAGE

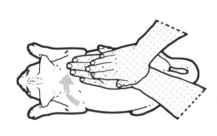

VIBRATION

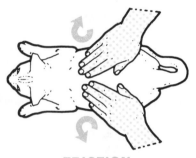

FRICTION

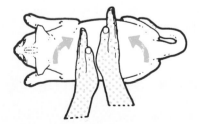

TAPOTEMENT

Shiatsu is an ancient Japanese methodology that involves the application of pressure (*atsu*) by the fingers (*shi*). Use only your fingers, thumbs, and palms to apply pressure to the various parts of the body in order to alleviate stiffness and keep the energy channels (*meridians*) clear. It is recommended that the individual receiving the treatment wear comfortable clothing.

FUN FACT ABOUT JAPAN: In Japan, it is considered inappropriate to blow your nose in public.

Rolfing, according to the Rolf Institute of Structural Integration, is "a holistic system of soft tissue manipulation and movement education that organize[s] the whole body in gravity." Only certified Rolfers can practice Rolfing, so I am legally prohibited from giving you specific instruction. But it's basically like being repeatedly flogged with a baseball bat.

NOTE: *Do not use Bengay or any other form of analgesic heat rub while performing your cat body massage.*

You have successfully completed Cat 101. You are now equipped with all fundamental, elementary, and rudimentary knowledge of Cat.

CAN I BRO HUG MY CAT?

No, you really shouldn't. While bro hugs are embraces demonstrating fraternal familiarity and admiration among male humans, they are best reserved for the pub, sporting arena, and casual business lunch. Your cat likes to be petted, so let's leave it at that.

FUN FACT ABOUT HUGGING: A normal hug lasts around 9.5 seconds. An abnormal hug lasts about three hundred hours.

CHAPTER 12

Roommate Issues

If you've followed all the steps so far, your cat should be easing into her new life and making herself comfortable in your (shared) home. But what do you do if she's making herself a little *too* comfortable?

She's sleeping on your bed, she's hogging the sofa, she's blocking the TV, she's on your computer (physically *on* your computer), she's using your toothbrush. . . . It's time to lay down some ground rules.

WHAT YOU CAN'T CHANGE

It's important to understand when dealing with your cat that no matter how hard you try, there are going to be certain things you're never going to be able to change, or convince your cat to change about himself. For example:

- **Your cat will never pay rent.** Although it might seem fair that your cat should at least chip in for all that it receives (the shelter, the food, the toys, the vacations), cats cannot understand the concept of money and don't have a viable way of earning and saving it. This is one of the big drawbacks of owning a cat, not unlike having a child, and it's just something you're going to have to accept as a mature cat owner.

- **Your cat will never clean up.** Where you see a "messy pile of clothes," your cat sees "a perfectly designed bed that smells like the guy who feeds me." Don't expect to come home and find the laundry done. On the plus side, your cat is fully capable of cleaning *itself*, so take that off your "to-do" list.

This doesn't mean you can't find a workable middle ground between you and your cat. You just need to be realistic about your expectations and consistent in your behavior.

SETTING BOUNDARIES

Your cat will naturally try to involve itself in all aspects of your life (unless he is feeling aloof, in which case you're on your own for a while). Setting boundaries consistently is the key to healthy cohabitation.

- **Set physical boundaries.** It's okay to have some space to yourself. If you want to be alone in your study, close the door. If your cat mews or scratches, try explaining to him (through the door) that there are many other rooms he can hang out in. Just be sure not to relent, even if he makes a fuss, or he'll know he can always wear you down.

IF THIS HAPPENS, YOUR PHYSICAL BOUNDARIES HAVE BEEN COMPROMISED

- **Set emotional boundaries.** Your cat's problems needn't become your problems. While you're responsible for some of his basic needs, he must learn to take ownership of his own happiness. He cannot expect you to solve everything for him. And if you feel yourself getting pulled into each and every one of his little problems, ask yourself: Are you indulging him because you *have* to? Or are you doing it because unconsciously you *want* to? Codependency is a slippery slope. These boundaries are as much for your well-being as his.

IF THIS HAPPENS, YOUR EMOTIONAL BOUNDARIES HAVE BEEN COMPROMISED

THE CHORE WHEEL

A time-tested technique for assigning easy-to-do tasks, the chore wheel will not only help keep the ship running smoothly, but will also give your cat a sense of responsibility and pride that he is "helping out" in even some small way. Tasks can include:

- Guarding the front window for several hours
- Checking the temperature of the bathroom floor with his belly
- Attacking bits of loose paper and string
- Patrolling various surfaces (table/counter/back of couch)
- Knocking things over (like cups and bottles)

Hey, you're a red-blooded man, you have desires, and you may, from time to time, have sleepover guests. An inquisitive cat can throw a wet blanket over the hottest of fires, but it's also your responsibility to give your cat the due notice he deserves. If you think it's going to be a special night, maybe suggest to him earlier in the day that he make some plans to hang out in the living room. And if you know you're going to be indisposed in the bedroom, try hanging a sock on the doorknob. It's a subtle but effective way to let him know that the boudoir is *ocupado* until further notice.

FUN FAKE CAT FACT: The movie *The Godfather* starring Marlon Brando was directed by a cat.

CHAPTER 13

Communication Issues

If you've made it this far, you are committed. You are in it for the long haul. But it won't always be easy. There will be squabbles and fights and differences of opinion. A lot of times you won't even understand her—or worse, you won't understand what *she's not saying*. How does she expect you to read her mind? Sometimes it's like she's speaking a different language. Luckily, science has brought our knowledge of feline communication to the point that, with a little practice, you can become a virtual Cat Whisperer.

MEOW MEANING

While Inuits have fifty words for snow, cats are mostly working with a lot of "meows." If you listen carefully, you'll know exactly what your little friend is trying to tell you.

CORDIAL

SHORT "MEOW" OR "MEW"

Greetings, e.g.:

- "Hello!"
- "Hey!"
- "Hey there."
- "Hi."
- "Hi there."
- "Wassup?"
- "Hi, just making sure you saw I'm here. I walked in, like, twenty minutes ago but you didn't say anything, so I thought I'd just say hi, how's it going?"

INQUISITIVE

MID-PITCHED "MEOW"

More of a question, e.g.:

- "What are you eating and can I have some or at least bug you about it?"
- "I noticed you moved the fern to where I can't get to it. Why?"
- "I was chewing on a rubber band near the sofa earlier today and . . . I think I might've swallowed it. Is that bad? Am I sick? Can you palpate my tonsils and make sure it's not stuck?"
- "Oh, you liked that nice mug, did you? It's too bad I swiped it with my tail and it broke into a thousand pieces, isn't it?"

MULTIPLE "MEOWS" OR "MEWS"

Excitement, e.g.:

- "I'm excited!"
- "Great to see you!"
- "You'll never guess how many things I knocked over today!"
- "I took the craziest nap ever today! It was almost sixteen hours long and I'm still tired!"
- "I'm just gonna keep making noise until you pet me or pick me up or something."

HYPER

DRAWN-OUT "MRRROOOOW"

A Demand with a capital *D*, e.g.:

- "I can't allow you to work on your computer or read that book so I'm going to obstruct your view!"
- "Open the door *now*! I need to be in the same room as you!"
- "I'm getting inside your sock drawer whether you like it or not!"

INTENT

LOW-PITCHED "MRRROOOOOWWW"

Complaint about a wrong you have done, e.g.:

- "Why did you invite your friends with the dog?!?!!"
- "I wasn't finished pawing that dead or dying mouse; return it to me at once, or else."
- "'Reduced-Calorie Formula for Feline Weight Control'? What are you trying to say to me?"

GLARING

HIGH-PITCHED "RRRROWW!"

Anger or pain, e.g.:

- *"You stepped on my tail!"*
- "When will racism not be a thing?!"
- "They canceled my favorite television program??? Noooooo!!!"
- "Give me back the goddamn fern!"

ALARMED

Cat body language is just as much an indicator of a cat's feelings and emotions as verbal discourse is. Pay attention to the following:

WHISKER POSITIONS

Pointed forward and fanning out = excited, intrigued, alert

Pressed flat against face = fearful, timid, sailing a boat and going really fast into a headwind

EAR POSITIONING

Erect, facing forward = content, relaxed

Flat against head = irritated, frightened, doing a *Miami Vice* look

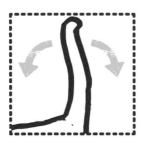

TAIL POSITIONING AND MOTION

Flicking back and forth = alert, interested

Wrapping around your leg = flirtatious, trying to trip you

KNEADING (AKA MAKING BISCUITS, AKA MAKING PIZZA DOUGH)

Feline flattery—she digs you, man!

Actually wants to make biscuits and is indicating to you that you need to go shopping for ingredients.

SQUINTING

Affectionate, relaxed, trusting

Is trying to read some small print and might need reading glasses

HAND ON HIP

Cocky, likely talking smack

FUN FAKE CAT FACT: America's third president Thomas Jefferson was one-eighth cat.

CHAPTER 14

What If My Cat's a Boy Cat? How to Bromance Your Cat

You say your cat is a boy cat? Right on, my man! It's gonna be dude central around your pad. You're about to cross a frat house with a zoo, with healthy doses of sports and roughhousing sprinkled on top for good measure. The entertainment possibilities with a boy cat are endless, but let's lay out a few of your top options to get you guys started.

INDOOR FUN

WATCH SPORTS WITH HIM

There's nothing like flopping on the couch with a couple tall ones, flipping on the sports channel, and catching a ball game with some buds. When your bud is also your faithful cat, it's that much more fun! Don't expect your cat to follow the subtleties of the infield fly rule, but if it's relaxed bro time you're looking for, catching a game is the way to go.

As fun as sports are on TV, nothing beats the roar of the crowd in person. Today's tickets will cost you a pretty penny, but seeing the big game live in person with your cat is something all guys should experience at least once. Your only major hurdle is finding a safe and successful way to smuggle your cat into the arena.

There are three options for maneuvering the smuggle:

Put your cat in a duffel bag but first make sure the duffel bag *does not look suspicious*. The last thing you want is for your cat duffel to be confiscated. You can easily neutralize the duffel's appearance by sticking a Canadian flag sticker on it. (This is especially recommended for hockey games.)

Stuff your cat inside your jacket and zip the jacket up to your neck. People will think that you've got a little bit of a lumpy tummy, but the shape and texture of your tummy is none of their beeswax so just ignore the sideways glances. Once you're seated unzip your jacket halfway to let your cat poke his head out and enjoy the game.

Wear your cat as a hat and play it super cool.

Can't get tickets to the game? Does your cat hate large crowds? Never fear, we've got you covered.

GRAB A BEER AT THE LOCAL PUB!

CATCH A TRUCK SHOW IF YOU'RE INTO THAT.

Really, *anything* you like to do on your own or with your human buddies, you can do with your cat buddy.

It's one thing to be a sports fan; it's quite another to be a sports-*man*. Here are some great outdoor activities for you and your cat to not just watch, but participate in as well.

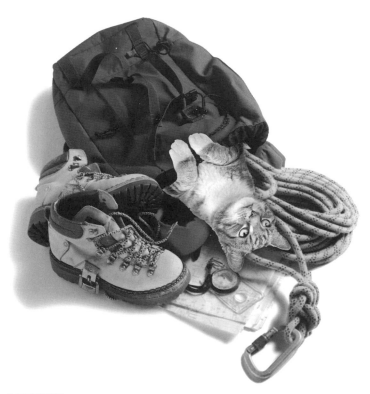

CAMPING!

Cats are not natural campers, but they'll do just fine. Really, nobody "likes" camping. It's just something you do one weekend a year. Why not share that weekend with your cat?

GOLFING!

You rarely see cats on the links, but remember: fifty years ago you rarely saw women or minorities golfing either. Times are changing and golf is a great way for your cat to work on his eye-paw coordination and get a great walking workout in.

Take your cat golfing—he can be your caddy.

HUNTING & FISHING!

Cats are natural predators, so why not take your cat fishing or hunting?

CAR SONGS

"Honky Cat"
ELTON JOHN

"What's New Pussycat?"
TOM JONES

"Cat's in the Cradle"
HARRY CHAPIN

"Faster Kill Pussycat"
PAUL OAKENFELD

"I Will Wait"
MUMFORD & SONS

FUN FAKE CAT FACT: Calico cats have the ability to speak French.

PARTYING WITH YOUR CAT

Pot for you, catnip for the cat. Easy as that! Catnip is a member of the mint family, and it gives cats a safe, nonaddictive buzz. The smell of it stimulates nerves in their brain.

Pot is marijuana, and it's great when you're really stressed out or tired or wired or bored. (Please consult your local authorities regarding the legality of marijuana possession and use, as the laws are changing from week to week.)

CHAPTER 15

What If My Cat's a Girl Cat? Becoming BFFs

You say your cat is a girl cat? OMG, do you even *realize* the journey of kinship and discovery you are about to embark upon? It's like the shelter *gave* you a sister to bring home and open your soul to. Let's take a look at some of the fun you two are going to have!

SPA DAY!

There is no better place to rejuvenate both the mind and the body than at a day spa. There's also no better place to spend the day with a bestie and catch up on all the dish! Spas are like amusement parks for people who like to lie around, so this will be nirvana for a dude like you and a cat like your cat. Just look at all the amenities a spa can offer:

Manicure, pedicure, facial, and, of course, a steam.

WORK OUT!

Getting in shape is usually a drag, but what if you could do it with your best friend?! Here are just a few ideas to get your mind racing and your heart pumping:

- Zumba
- Spinning
- Pilates
- The Barre Method

SHOPPING!

Have credit card, will travel! Just make sure you have a big enough Frappuccino to get you through!

HANG TIME!

The goal is to spend some QT with your best friend, so remember— you don't *have* to go out anywhere. Pour a couple glasses of Malbec, settle on the couch, and just spend a few hours reconnecting. By the end you'll be asking each other, "Why don't we do this more often?"

CHAPTER 16

Hair and Fashion

Now that you've mastered the basics of cat ownership, it's time to have a little fun. Your cat isn't just your new best friend and a symbol of your growth as a man. He's also a beautiful animal that deserves to be admired by the world. Your cat's defining feature is, of course, his beautiful coat of fur. Let's examine it and see what the possibilities are, not just for health and maintenance, but even perhaps a little pizzazz.

WHY DO CATS SHED SO MUCH?

Shedding is a natural process for most cats; it allows them to moderate their body temperature at different times of the year. If you lived outdoors with your cat, you'd barely notice the shedding. It's only because the cat is indoors and sitting on your new brushed-suede love seat that you even notice it.

If the shedding is becoming an annoyance, you can talk to your cat about stepping outside when he needs to shed, but it's probably better just to accept the slight inconvenience and stay on top of your cleaning. I recommend twice-a-week vacuuming and keeping a supply of lint rollers for spot cleanups.

Anxious cats may also shed more than normal, so if you feel that the fur piles are abnormal, talk to your cat and see if anything's eating at him. And, of course, older cats may just be naturally losing their hair, a condition known as "male-cattern baldness."

Short-haired cats are stuck with what the good Lord gave them. But if you have a long-haired cat that's looking to stand out on the scene, you can totally style this one to rock out.

FOR THE BOYS . . .

INDIE ROCK SHAG

FAUXHAWK

JUSTIN
BIEBER HAIR

HIPSTER BANGS

EIGHTIES
ANGULAR

PIGTAILS

Whatever style you choose, *don't* pull the hair too tight. Cats hate that, and the resulting scowl of displeasure will ruin even the coolest looks. Do pet your cat's fur.

FASHION

If there's one thing we can all agree cats love, it's fashion and looking fashionable. Even a cursory Google image search on "cats" and "fashion" shows pages upon pages of dolled-up cats giving their very best model pouts.

How you decide to dress your cat is up to you, though your cat definitely has "veto power" (claws) if he or she feels your "couture" isn't so "haute." Here is a starter list of clothing staples and accessories that you can mix and match to help you and your cat find the style that works for both of you:

- Jeans
- Jean shorts
- Corduroy vest
- Moon boots
- V-neck sweater
- Triple F.A.T. goose-down jacket
- Tricornered hat
- *Eyes Wide Shut* sex mask
- Air Jordans
- Sweatpants
- Watermelon costume
- Disney World Magic Mountain commemorative
- T-shirt
- Jockey briefs
- Unitard
- Brooklyn Nets baseball cap
- Hooded sweatshirt (no zipper)
- Ice skates
- Swim goggles
- Vintage Benetton rugby jersey
- Poncho
- Swatch watch
- Uggs
- Bow tie (any color)

CAN I GIVE MY CAT A BATH?

No. Don't do that.

CHAPTER 17

Introducing Your Cat to Humans, and Other Animals

By this point you and your cat are likely spending a *lot* of time together. And while that intense, almost unnatural connection will help you greatly in eventually becoming a true Cat Lady Guy, it's important for your cat to interact with others from time to time, if only to reaffirm his belief that the world outside the little cocoon you have created is too chaotic and unpredictable and only you can truly protect him (which is the truth). Let's take a look at some of the people and animals your cat might meet, and try to anticipate any problems that might arise.

HEY I WANT YOU TO MEET SOMEONE.

I'M TIRED.

YOUR CAT AND CHILDREN

It is conventional wisdom that cats don't like children. The truth is that they actually like children just as much as they like anyone else, which is of course not terribly much. Nonetheless, it's important for your cat to be exposed to children. As a well-rounded man you may someday want children of your own, and your cat is going to need to know how to tolerate or at least successfully hide from them. Find a friend with kids, invite the clan over, and let your cat experience the wonder of toddlers.

YOUR CAT AND OLD PEOPLE

Cats are naturally drawn to the elderly. Old people are kind, they move slowly, and they often smell vaguely of fish. Why not bring your cat to the local home for the elderly and make some old people's day? And it's not just for the elderly—your cat will be thrilled to spend some QT with a group of people who sleep as much as *she* does.

"MY SISTER IS AFRAID OF MY CAT!"

YOUR CAT FREAKS ME OUT, MAKE IT GO AWAY.

Maybe it's not your sister. Maybe it's your brother. Or a nephew. But there will inevitably be someone in your family who claims that cats "frighten" them. Don't waste your time trying to redeem cats in general for this person. Just try to show your sister or brother or nephew that there's nothing to fear with *your* little guy. Maybe dress your cat up in a little clown suit to illustrate just how goofy and nonthreatening he is.[4]

I JUST MOWED THE LAWN.

WHO WANTS LEMONADE?

"MY CAT IS AFRAID OF MY FATHER!"

Well, your father can be an intimidating presence. Remember, your cat is taking his cues from you in these situations. Ask yourself this: Is it really your cat that has an issue with your father? Or is it you? When was the last time you sat down and really reconnected with your dad? Does he even know that you can pick locks now? Don't let the inertia of modern family life rob you of quality time with your father. Someday that time will be gone, and you'll wish like hell that you could get it back.

---

4   Best-case scenario is a clown suit with a flower boutonniere that squirts water.

WOOF

CATS AND DOGS

There's an expression, "fighting like cats and dogs," that suggests the two species are naturally antagonistic toward each other. However, there's also the expression "It's raining cats and dogs," which doesn't really mean *anything*. Another expression is that "a stitch in time saves nine," which means that if you put a stitch in time it will save you nine. The point is, there are exceptions to every rule, but I would recommend keeping your cat away from dogs.

CATS AND FROGS

Unless your cat is a Louisiana frog cat, cats mostly don't even know what a frog is or that they exist, so don't stress about this one too much.

CATS AND OTHER CATS

Have you ever stepped up to a craps table while in Nevada and "rolled the bones"? Well, that's what you're doing when your cat meets another cat. They might be immediate best friends and snuggle up into a little circle of fur to nap. But they might also get all gladiator on each other. Maybe show your cat some pictures of this new cat and see how he responds before setting up a playdate.

FUN FAKE CAT FACT: The Alaskan crab cat is ½ crab and ½ cat.

WHY IS MY CAT SO SHY?

Why are you so shy at dinner parties? Why are you so bad at
Donkey Kong? We are what we are, man. Some cats are natural
extroverts. Others, like yours, may just prefer to watch the show
from the back of the room. There's nothing wrong with being shy.
J. D. Salinger, for example, was a notorious shut-in, and look what
he did.[5] Maybe if you stopped being such an overbearing stage
mom and let him explore the world at his own pace he wouldn't
be so anxious about dipping his toe in the stream of life. You've
got *your* life—let him have his. It's only when you are both fulfilled
separately that you can truly make each other happy together.

5   He wrote books.

CHAPTER 18

Shopping for Two

You aren't just a dude anymore. You are a caretaker. It's time to get real, my man.

Your old shopping list probably looked something like this:

- Barbecue sauce
- Shampoo
- Milk
- Soy sauce
- Microwavable meatballs
- Bacon
- Band-Aids
- Extra barbecue sauce and shampoo

Not only did the above not provide for a cat's needs, it was also not particularly nutritious and hardly provided for *your* needs, and, furthermore, it kind of grossed people out. You need to invest in your own health so your cat has a strong partner in you. Remember: your cat has nine lives,6 and you better keep up.

Your new shopping list should look like this:

- *Vegetables* (there are many kinds)
- *Fruits* (also many kinds)
- *Whole grains* (go crazy, the healthy way!)
- *Lean protein* (your arteries will thank you later)
- Dry cat food
- Wet cat food
- Cat treats
- Milk replacement
- Eyedrops for cats
- Digestive enzymes and probiotics for cats
- Joint Complete for cats
- Antianxiety and antistress homeopathic supplement for cats
- Kitty litter (odor free)
- Squeaky toy
- Alternate squeaky toy
- String (if there's one central tenet of this book it is this: *you can never have too much string*)

Don't forget to bring your reusable shopping bag along with you to the store—let's leave a better planet behind for our cats!!!

---

6   Again, this is merely a popular theory and has not yet been proven.

CHAPTER 19

Your Cat, the Ultimate Wingman

You didn't get a cat to help you chase women. You got a cat because you'd become the man you wanted to be and felt ready to share that evolution in a positive way with the world around you. But the fact remains: your cat gives you a distinct advantage in the dating world, and it's one you need to exploit. Your cat is a perfect wingman. Let's look at how you two can work together to land the babes.

IMPRESSING GIRLS WITH YOUR CAT

Women are drawn to men who show an ability to protect and nurture. All the qualities you've developed by caring for your cat are a flashing sign to women that says "Scoop this guy up before someone else does!" The trick is to let them see that nurturing side. I recommend strapping your cat into a BabyBjörn carrier and bringing him out for an afternoon of errands. Don't worry about finding women. They will find you. Just care about your cat as you always do and let the rest just happen.

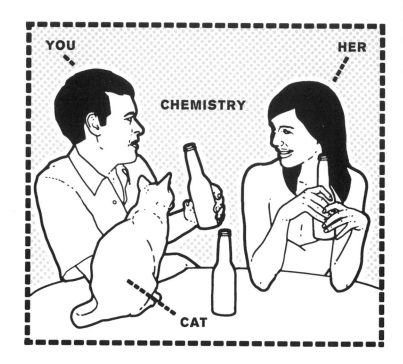

PICKUP LINES INVOLVING YOUR CAT

Even if you've left your cat at home, his presence in your life and the important role he plays provide endless opportunities to bait the hook and reel in the ladies. Here are just a few examples of lines you might try:

"I'd love for you to meet my cat, I think he'd find you purrrrfect!"

"I don't know about you, but I'm 'feline' like getting a drink. May I buy you one?"

"You don't have a boyfriend? You gotta be 'kitten' me! [pause] That's a joke I like to make with my cat. I'm a very passionate cat owner."

"I'm total suburban-dad material. I like to meow the lawn."

If you're really looking to "own the night" and impress the ladies, there is simply no better play than to bring your cat out with you on the town. (An infant works great too, of course, but the logistics of feeding and changing a newborn in a dance club generally outweigh the positives.)

Women may be intimidated at being approached by both you and your cat simultaneously. Your baller play is to approach a woman by yourself and, after a couple minutes or a nonverbal signal, have your cat sidle up to you two from the other side. When the young lady jumps in fear/surprise, just say casually, "Oh, that's just my cat," and slip him a little skin. If she sticks around after that introduction, you are golden. (Just don't forget to put the sock on your doorknob when you get home!)

YOUR CAT AS YOUR GET-OUT-OF-JAIL-FREE CARD

Your cat is also a valuable tool for extricating yourself from unpleasant dating/flirtation situations without all the normal social awkwardness. If you are flying solo at the club and stuck talking to a dead-ender, you can always use the old "I've got to go home and feed my cat his diabetes medication" line (white lie at worst, sad truth at best).

If your cat is there with you, have your cat jump up on the bar and begin plaintively meowing in your face. You guys will have to have agreed on your "parts" in this scene, but the gist should be that your cat is tired and wants to leave, while *you* want to stay but you feel an obligation to your cat. Your cat says, "I'm going to wait in the car," and walks away; then all you have to do is gesture toward the door apologetically, say your good-byes, and you're home free. It's like war out there in the dating world . . . you'd be a fool to head into battle without a weapon like your cat by your side.

- Guy persona and cat persona are intrinsically linked.

- Name your cat something spunky, and be as original as you want to be.

- Spay and neuter. Don't think about it: just do it.

- To avoid injury when lifting and holding your cat, lift from your core and legs rather than your lower back.

- To avoid injury when petting your cat, do not make direct eye contact at first. This is considered confrontational. Instead, hold your face at a three-quarters angle away from the cat's gaze.

- Living with a cat can be challenging, but honesty and compromise are the best policies.

- Cats meow.

- Be bros with your boy cat and BFFs with your girl cat.

- Bathe your cat only when absolutely necessary.

- Learn how to flirt effectively from your cat. He should know—he's quite the flirt himself.

YOU MUST BE A BAKER BECAUSE THOSE ARE THE HOTTEST BUNS I'VE EVER SEEN.

Free-write in the blank space provided about what it means to be a cat caretaker. Be honest. You may be surprised by what you write.

Being a cat caretaker means . . .

CAT LADY PROGRESS REPORT #2:
CAN YOU IDENTIFY YOURSELF?

Which individual best resembles you?

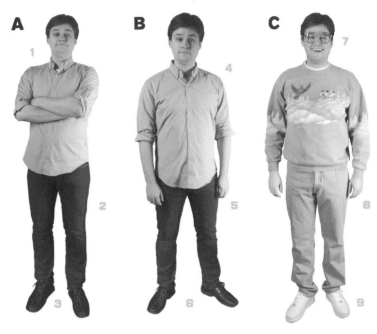

1. Small amount of cat hair
2. Cell phone in pocket with photos of you and your friends hanging out (maybe one cat picture, out of focus)
3. Comfortable shoes suitable for indoor and outdoor use
4. A profound lack of cat hair
5. Cell phone in pocket with pictures of you engaged in your active social life
6. Shoes perfect for leaving your home or apartment in because you have things to do
7. Dark circles under eyes from a few sleepless nights involving your cat, a full moon, and some crazy wall shadows
8. Cell phone containing 7Gbs worth of pictures of your cat
9. Cat pee on your shoe that you don't even know is there

If you chose A—Former Self—then you need to reread Part Two.

If you chose B—Former-Former Self—then you need to re-reread Parts One and Two.

If you selected C—Cat Person—*well done!* You are on your way. With Intermediate Cat under your belt, you have only a few credits left until you've achieved your full certification!

The last phase in your education: Advanced Cat. It's time to get out of the classroom and into the lab. This is a hands-on practicum, and truthfully, not everyone is cut out for the challenging fieldwork. It's one thing to simply take care of a cat—it's another to let the cat *take care of you.* More than a lifestyle choice, this is a Way of Life, period. This is the Wisdom of Cat. Listen to the Cat. What is her Dharma? Listen . . . shh . . . She is your Guru. . . .

Only once you are able to transcend from standard cat person to celebrated Cat Lady Guy will your education be complete. You must learn to serve the Cat so that she may serve you. It is a mutualistic, symbiotic relationship in its purest form. You live with each other—*and you live* for *each other.*

At times you will curse the Path. "It's too hard! I'm covered in scratches, my carpet smells like pee, and no humans will hang out with me." *Stay the course.*

Yes, you *can* incorporate the Cat Lady life into your Guy life. Thus far you have transformed from schlubby nobody to Somebody with a Cat. Now the work becomes: Somebody *and* a Cat. Good luck!

GAMES + PUZZLES

REALLY HARD SUDOKU

VIRTUALLY IMPOSSIBLE SUDOKU

7

3

CONNECT THE DOTS

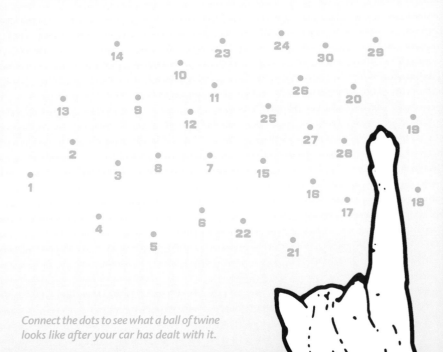

Connect the dots to see what a ball of twine looks like after your car has dealt with it.

CAT LADY BRAIN TEASER

*"In my house, the number of cats
who do wear a collar
is double the number of cats
who don't wear a collar.
But the number of dogs in my house
who do not wear a collar
is double the number of dogs who do.*

*"If I tell you the number of cats
in my house
is double the number of dogs,
can you tell me the number of cats
I have? Here's a clue:
more than 20; less than 32!"*

A: *24 cats (just the right amount!).*

BRAIN TEASERS

Q: *The recipe for your cat's favorite type of cat food requires 2¼ cups of tuna for 5 servings. You need enough tuna for 8 servings. How much tuna will you need?*

A: *Turns out the cat doesn't want to eat tuna today.*

Q: *Your cat loves knocking over the lamp on your desk and can successfully do it 65% of the time. If he tries to knock the lamp over 30 times, how many times will he succeed?*

A: *Enough times for you to get upset about it.*

WORD JUMBLE

Unscramble the following four words. Use one letter from each word to form another familiar word.

R S I H S K W E

G S I T N R

U S C I R O Y T I

P C I N A T

CAT

COVERED
IN FUR

COMMUNICATE
IN MEOWS

MARK
TERRITORY BY
SPRAYING
EVERYWHERE

CAT GUY

LIKE TO SLEEP

LIKE RUBBING SELVES
AGAINST GIRLS

EAT ANYTHING

PEE STANDING UP

DON'T UNDERSTAND
RULES TO COMPETITIVE
FIGURE SKATING

GUY

PARTIALLY
COVERED IN FUR

COMMUNICATE
IN GRUNTS

MARK
TERRITORY
BY LEAVING
LAUNDRY
EVERYWHERE

DID YOU KNOW . . . ?

- Calico cats are almost always female.
- Cats' nose pads are uniquely ridged, like human fingerprints.
- Cats' brains are physiologically more similar to humans' brains than dogs' brains are.
- Cats can be left-pawed or right-pawed.
- Cats walk on their toes.

FUN FAKE CAT FACT: The capital of Ohio is called Kitty Cat. It's named after a cat.

"You can never have too many framed photos of your kitties or too many a-meow-zing holiday sweaters."

"For a quick weeknight treat, try this: pick up a nice piece of line-caught trout at the fish market, smoke it in your outdoor smoker, let it sit overnight so the flavors really come together, retrieve it in the morning, drop it in the blender, puree until smooth, and serve in a discarded can. Bon appétit, kitties!"

"Did you know there are a lot of good deals in the Penny Saver? It's true. There are."

MORE

ASK MIKE!

GREAT QUESTIONS,
I'LL GET BACK
TO YOU

"My dog comes when I call his name, but my cat won't come when I call hers. Why?"

I hear you, man. Cats are weird like that.

"Does my cat actually love me, or is her affection a smokescreen?"

She loves you but in a "I love you cuz you feed me" sorta way.

"What's the deal with politicians? Will they ever get along?"

One can only hope. Politics is very frustrating.

"Is astrology for real? I'm a Libra and I totally don't think that fits."

OMG. You are SO totally a Libra.

"My friend Andy's cat has thumbs. Why?"

Andy must have a Tennessee Thumb Cat.

"How come when I ask my cat a question he doesn't respond?"

In all likelihood because he doesn't know the answer.

"My dog catches a Frisbee in her mouth. When I throw a Frisbee at my cat, he just moves out of the way. How come?"

Your cat probably doesn't enjoy playing Frisbee. Have you tried lawn darts or croquet?

TOP EIGHT PUBLIC FIGURES WHO LOOK LIKE CATS

- Cate Blanchett
- Anderson Cooper
- Steve Buscemi
- Taylor Swift
- Charo
- President William Taft
- David Bowie
- James Carville

SPORTS FRANCHISES NAMED AFTER CATS

- Cubs
- Tigers
- Lions
- Bengals
- Jaguars
- Bobcats

MUSICIANS AND BANDS NAMED AFTER CATS

- Cat Power
- Cat Stevens
- Stray Cats
- John Cougar Mellencamp
- Pussycat Dolls
- White Lion
- Def Leppard
- Glass Tiger

Just because you're obsessed with cats doesn't mean every movie you own has to be about them. Just most of them. . . . These are all rated G:

Felix the Cat: The Movie (1989)

A Cat's Tale (2008)

The Cat from Outer Space (1978)

The Cat Returns (2002)

The Lion King II: Simba's Pride (1998)

Homeward Bound: The Incredible Journey (1993)

The Adventures of Milo and Otis (1989)

That Darn Cat (1965)

The Aristocats (1970)

Oliver and Company (1988)

FUN FAKE CAT FACT: The original drummer for the Beatles before Ringo was a cat.

TV is something you and your cat can do together. These shows are for both of you, so keep an open mind when considering them:

My Cat from Hell (Animal Planet)

Must Love Cats (Animal Planet)

Cats 101 (Animal Planet)

Top Cat (Hanna-Barbera)

Eek! The Cat (Fox Kids)

Tom and Jerry (Hanna-Barbera)[7]

Slacker Cats (ABC Family)

The Garfield Show (Cartoon Network)

Heathcliff (DIC Entertainment)

Perry Mason, "The Case of the Careless Kitten" (CBS)

7   Beware, comical violence.

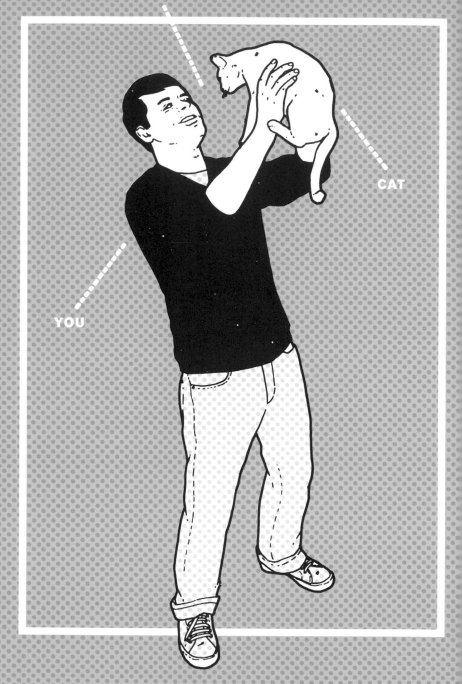

PART THREE

ADVANCED CAT

Think about how far you've come since you started reading my book. When you first skimmed the table of contents you were a knuckle-dragging Neanderthal who didn't know an Oriental Long-hair from a kick to the head. And look at you now: you're a cat owner and a cat lover. You can pet, feed, dress, even bro out with your cat. Your cat has made you a better man, and vice versa.

But slow down, partner, you're still not a Cat Lady. Not yet, anyway.

To really take your cat obsession to the next level, to transform this from the "most important relationship in your life" to the "all-consuming only relationship in your life," you'll have to master the lessons ahead. You may not feel ready for these challenges. Frankly, you may not be. But if you are truly committed to becoming a Cat Lady, this is the road you must travel. Buckle up, friend. Let's finish the journey.

CHAPTER 20

Cat Cribs

Your cat shares your home. Why not let your home reflect that? What better way to show your new life partner your commitment to this intense relationship than to turn your bachelor pad into a real, HARD-CORE CAT PAD?

Designing a legit cat crib takes more than a supply of catnip and some "Hang In There!" posters. You need commitment to a vision and the determination to see it through. These are bold choices, but you are ready.

OPTION #1: PIMP OUT YOUR CAT CRIB

If your cat is from the streets or has acquired any kind of comparable "cred," the Pimp-Out is the way to go.

Our interior decorator's artistic rendering of the Pimp-Out:

- We built a *center console* out of onyx to house your cat's strings, balls, and other toys.
- We hooked up a *video monitor* in the coffee table that plays a continuous loop of whatever most stimulates your cat: fish swimming, squirrels darting, lasers pointing, empty box beckoning, etc.

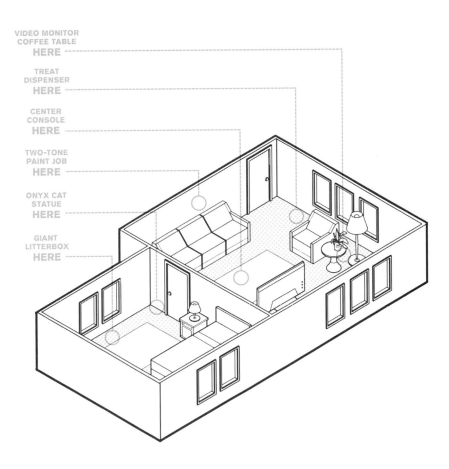

VIDEO MONITOR
COFFEE TABLE
HERE

TREAT
DISPENSER
HERE

CENTER
CONSOLE
HERE

TWO-TONE
PAINT JOB
HERE

ONYX CAT
STATUE
HERE

GIANT
LITTERBOX
HERE

- Your cat loves treats, so we installed a *cat treat dispenser* made out of onyx inside this antique wooden coatrack.
- *Chiquitas* (and cats) like a body that's buff, so we re-buffed this *onyx obelisk* and chiseled a seated *statue in your cat's likeness.*
- We hit these walls with a calico-inspired *two-tone paint job.*
- We know how cats love a big litter box, so we turned your bedroom into an *enormous litter box* made out of onyx.

Is your cat more of a lover than a fighter? The soft-spoken, introspective type? Help her reconnect with her inner qi (pronounced "chee") and tap in to the subtle but profound energies of the universe by crafting a harmonious sanctuary.

Balance between yin properties and yang properties is a key aspect to achieving feng shui in your personal space. For two parts yin, it is ideal to adopt two parts yang, and so on. Think of you and your cat as "yin" and "yang": powerful forces, often at odds, inextricably linked in the furious dance of life.

Our Feng Shui consultant's brainstorm for the Feng Shui-Out:

- Both your bed and your cat's bed should be arranged so that your feet and your cat's feet are *never pointing directly at the door*. Position your bed and the cat's bed against a wall to achieve an optimal sense of grounding. If your cat's bed is your bed, then that's one less puzzle to solve!
- Your bedroom will need to be a *west-facing space* to accommodate your cat's night owl tendencies, so you may have to knock down a wall or purchase the adjoining unit in your condo. It's worth it.
- Clear that clutter! Chaos blocks energy flow, so urge your cat to put all her belongings away in her *designated storage containers* at the end of the night.
- Remove unnecessary gadgets and electronics, like extra cordless shaver charging stations and that theremin you're never going to learn to play. These devices emit currents that disrupt sleep—and we all know how much your cat needs sleep!

Plants promote serenity in your living space. The following plants are poisonous to cats, so select *anything but these*:

Aloe vera
Amaryllis
Cactus
Calla lily
Charming dieffenbachia
Chinese evergreen
Chrysanthemum
Daffodil
Delphinium
Devil's ivy
Dicentra
Dieffenbachia dumb cane
Easter lily
Elephant ears
English ivy
Eucalyptus
Ferns
Geranium
German ivy

Giant dumb cane
Hahn's self-branching ivy
Heartleaf philodendron
Indian rubber plant
Lily
Mistletoe
Mother-in-law's tongue
Peace lily
Philodendron
Plumosa fern
Poinsettia
Rhododendron
Rubber plant
Saddle leaf philodendron
Satin pothos
Spotted dumb cane
Sweetheart ivy
Tropic snow dieffenbachia

Your relationship with your cat is the most important thing in your life, and your apartment should reflect that. And nothing else. This option requires that you throw a lot of stuff out, so you may want to invest in steel-lined "pro-style" garbage bags or perhaps even one of those "Bagsters" from Waste Management that are so popular these days.

A GREAT WAY TO THROW AWAY YOUR LIFE!

The first step is to remove any obvious clutter, both physical and emotional. Begin by throwing out bulky furniture and personal memories. These may include:

- High school and/or college yearbook
- Sofa
- Easy chair
- Family photos
- Coffee table
- Bed
- Letters your grandfather wrote to your grandmother during World War II
- Workout bench
- Childhood blanket you've kept in a special box for thirty years
- Your baby teeth

From what remains, make a pile of only the things relevant to your life *right* now—things you absolutely need to survive. These may include:

- Your cat
- Your cat's litter box
- Your cat's food and whatever you serve the food in
- Toys to entertain your cat
- Books to read to your cat
- A digital camera or smartphone to take photos of your cat
- Internet service to upload cat photos
- One mattress, one pillow, no sheets (do you really need more? does your cat?)

Everything else can go. Everything else is a distraction from the main event, which is the magic between you and your cat.

Whichever choice you make when reenvisioning your home space, be bold. Why not take a chance? Look at the leap of faith you took with this furry friend, and look how far it has taken you! Did you do it? Great! You're on your way.

CHAPTER 21

Stepping Into the World

Now that you and your cat have mastered your domain, it's time to take this crazy, against-all-odds show on the road and share with the world the special bond you two have built. Stepping out of the home may mean stepping outside of your and/or your cat's comfort zone, but you didn't come this far to shy away from difficult but rewarding shared experiences, did you? Plus, if you don't explore the world outside your home with your cat, you'll never be able to realize that the world is a crazy, dangerous place that doesn't "get" you guys and never has and maybe it's best if you two just stayed cooped up where it's safe until one or both of you dies or is evicted for violating health codes. Let's explore the world!

TAKING YOUR CAT TO WORK

Your coworkers bring their babies, their bigger children, and sometimes even their dogs in to work. Why should they have all the fun? Bring your cat! He'll love the chance to explore an exciting new world of chairs, computers, filing cabinets, and pants legs. You'll enjoy his company and save a bundle on the remote home "cat monitoring system" you would have had to install to achieve any peace of mind when leaving him at home. Here are some helpful tips to make the occasion a success:

- Cats love to explore new spaces on their own terms and in their own time, so when bringing your cat to work, show up early (four or five a.m.) to give him a few hours to find his comfort zone.

- Set up a "cat office" underneath your desk for your guy, and make sure he's got enough to keep him occupied during your nine-to-five.

- Station a litter box near the water cooler.

- Be sure to introduce your cat to everyone during lunch.

- Bring your cat to a staff meeting so that he can see what your work life is all about.

- If you are brought in for an HR hearing about bringing your cat to work, make sure you bring your cat to the hearing. It's important to have a witness and advocate at these kinds of meetings.

You work hard building a life for you and your cat and you're going to need some R&R to recharge your batteries. Make sure you plan vacations for you and your cat at least twice a year. I'm not talking about a day trip hiking in the Catskills. I'm talking about six days/five nights, with a nice hotel and a flight and all the excitement and relaxation that comes with traveling domestically or abroad with your cat.

TRAVEL TIPS:

- *Pack for your cat.* Your cat may insist on packing his own bag, but cats are notoriously bad "planners." Make sure you oversee his packing. If you're going skiing, make sure he brings his goggles. If you're heading to the Caribbean, don't let him forget his sun hat.

- *Prepare for jet lag.* You know how important sleep is to your cat. Disrupted sleep patterns due to travel can derail even the most relaxing vacation. If you are traveling across more than two time zones, add at least three days to the trip to allow your cat to adjust his internal clock. He may also need an additional week of downtime upon return to get back in the groove.

- *Choose a cat-friendly resort.* Your vacation won't be relaxing if it's up to you to entertain your cat the entire time. If you have the option to choose a hotel or resort that specializes in cat activities and entertainment, find that extra scratch and pay the premium. Your cat will thank you when he comes back from his special beachside cat trampolining class!

I LIKE TO
HIDE IN BAGS.

DESTINATIONS:

The world is a big place and there are countless fun destinations, but here are a few of my favorites when traveling with my cat:

- Napa Valley, California
- Puerto Rico
- Branson, Missouri
- Istanbul, Turkey
- Barcelona, Spain
- Martha's Vineyard
- Cancún, Mexico (off-season: avoid spring break)
- Edinburgh, Scotland (go for the Fringe Festival!)
- Cape Town, South Africa
- New York City
- Providence, Rhode Island
- Kyoto, Japan
- Luxembourg
- Pittsburgh, Pennsylvania
- Reno, Nevada (especially if your cat's a gambler!)

STAY-CATIONS WITH YOUR CAT

Not everyone has the money for big trips these days, but that doesn't mean you can't "get away from it all" while staying right where you are. If your budget is tight, maybe a "stay-cation" is what you and your cat need. Here are a few tips to make your Plan B feel like an adventurous Plan A:

- *Pretend you're somewhere exotic.* Your home could easily be a bungalow in the jungles of Costa Rica if you make sure to not look out your windows, so use your imagination and make it so! Talk with your cat about the beauty of the local foliage. Worry excessively about the potability of the tap water from your sink. Wonder why housekeeping hasn't come by to change your sheets and towels.

- *Go camping in your yard.* There's plenty to explore right outside your home or apartment. Set up a tent in your backyard or apartment complex's parking lot and spend a night or two learning all the sounds your home makes from the *outside*!

- *Visit the airport.* Too often we take the fun and excitement of the airport for granted because we're rushing *through* it to go somewhere else. Why not spend a day touring your airport with your cat and enjoying all that it offers? Your cat will love watching the planes take off and land. And while you're there, why not treat yourselves to a Cinnabon cinnamon roll and hot chocolate? Just because you're staying close to home doesn't mean you can't live like kings!

The important thing to remember is that whatever you're doing—whether at work, on vacation, or at home—you're doing it with your number-one and now probably only friend, your cat. As long as you two are together, does anything else really even matter? And if no one else understands, do you even care?

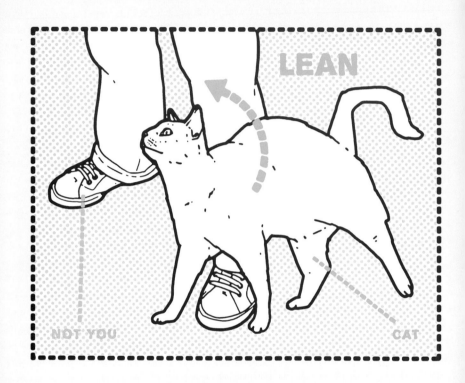

CHAPTER 22

Five Ways to Tell If Your Cat Is Rubbing Itself on Someone Else's Leg

Almost half of American marriages end in divorce. Of those, the average length of a marriage is a mere eight years. You and your cat will be together an average of thirteen years. So yeah, there are going to be some bumps in the road.

When your cat rubs against your leg, it is a special form of intimacy that says, "Hey you. You're here." Sadly, sometimes your cat will search out that intimacy outside the home or, even worse, with someone else *inside* your home. If you think you've got a straying cat on your hands, ask yourself these questions:

1. Is your cat not rubbing itself on you as much as it normally does?
2. Does your cat smell like someone other than your cat or you?
3. Do you know someone who has been in your home recently and whose pants appear to be covered in cat hair?
4. Has your cat been acting completely uninterested in you lately?
5. Is your cat rubbing itself on someone else's leg?

If you answered yes to any of these, then your cat is probably rubbing itself on someone else's leg.

Fear not—this isn't the end for you and your cat. Your cat will rub itself on many things in your lifetime together: men's legs, women's legs, chair legs, table legs—maybe even a peg leg, if given the opportunity. You can make that cat your cat, but you can never make it *not* a cat. And a cat's gonna rub whatever leg is closest. It's part of the price of admission, my friend.

Your cat still loves you, and nothing can change that. (You feed it.) Busy yourself with another activity while your cat is off doing other things to other people's legs. Hey, now is a great time to get reacquainted with your old electronic gaming system or a similar interest of times past. Or if you have a special person in your life, plan a little QT together, at least until this situation blows over.

DON'T WORRY, YOU'RE STILL MY FAVORITE PERSON TO PESTER FOR FOOD.

CHAPTER 23

Are You Spending Too Much Time with Your Cat?

Sounds like a crazy question, doesn't it? But take a step back and consider the following.

ARE YOU NEGLECTING YOUR FAMILY?

When was the last time you spoke to your parents on the phone?

Did you end the conversation by saying, "You guys are boring, I'm going to go hang with my cat"?

Open up your visual memory bank: are you having trouble remembering your brother's face?

Wait, do you even *have* a brother?

You may be neglecting your family.

Did you skip the company picnic for a photo shoot with your cat?

Does the autoreply message on your e-mail read, "I can't respond to your message right now because I'm home playing with my cat"?

Do you Skype with your cat while at work?

Do you badger your employees to follow your cat on Twitter?

How many unanswered e-mails do you have?

And dating back how far?

Open up your visual memory bank: are you having trouble placing your boss's face?

Do you even remember what you do for a living?

You may be neglecting your job.

FUN CAT FACT: When a cat's owner dies, the cat will wait up to ten minutes out of loyalty before finding a new human to feed and protect him or her.

ARE YOU NEGLECTING YOUR FRIENDS?

Think back: when was the last time you went out for a drink with the guys?

Did you bring your cat with you?

Do you mistakenly call all your friends' wives by your cat's name?

Have you ever skipped a bar crawl because you just wanted to stay home and listen to your cat purr?

Have you ever taken your cat out with you so you could listen to her purr while on a pub crawl?

Do you divert the conversation so that you can talk about your cat?

When you *do* see your friends, does your brain shut off if the conversation isn't in some way cat related?

Do you not have any friends anymore?

You may be neglecting your friends.

However, even if you *are* neglecting family, friends, and work, that *in no way* means you are spending too much time with your cat. It's really impossible to spend too much time with your cat, and since he definitely "gets" you better than all the fakers and frauds out there, he's really the one you need to stay focused on. Jobs come and go, family will always take you back, friends are . . . whatever. You're becoming a Cat Lady Guy. Sacrifices come with the territory.

CHAPTER 24

Could You Possibly Spend More Time with Your Cat?

I mean, sure! Why not? We've already established that you can't be spending *too much* time with your cat, so a little more can't possibly hurt.

Here are some terrific ways you can spend more time with your cat:

- Start an a cappella group with your cat and some of her friends
- Start a band with your cat
- Start a business with your cat
- Join a gym with your cat (look into family memberships to save money)
- Pitch a reality show to the networks about you and your cat
- Go big-game hunting with your cat
- Just sit around and stare at your cat while she sleeps
- Form a two-person long-form improv troupe
- Invent some newfangled workout regimen together and get rich on DVD sales
- Take up archery (your cat won't be able to handle a bow, but she can carry the quiver if you strap it to her back)
- Organize a neighborhood patrol with your cat and nearby pets
- Make a pilgrimage to the flagship Olive Garden in Orlando, Florida
- Start a YouTube channel with your cat

- Volunteer with your cat
- Learn a foreign language with your cat
- Train for a half marathon with your cat
- Take an adult education course with your cat
- Sit down with your cat and finally write that novel you've always talked about
- Meditate with your cat
- Build something with your cat—anything! When's the last time you built something with your own two hands?

Pretty much anything you might do on your own or with other people, you can do with your cat. Isn't a shared life fulfilling?

CHAPTER 25

Toughing It Out

Raising a cat is much like raising a child—it's a uniquely reward-ing experience that will at times test you to your core. You want your cat to be okay. You want your cat to be safe. You want your cat to always love you. But you guys are going to go through some tough times (and I'm not just talking about him rubbing a stray leg or two). There will be fights, and tears, and some very real-world dangers. This ain't Candy Land. This is life.

FIGHTING WITH YOUR CAT

You don't *want* to fight with your cat. Half the time, you probably don't even remember later what started the conflict in the first place. Maybe your cat left her poop uncovered in the litter box one too many times. Or maybe *she* got tired of *you* tsk-tsking her fashion choices when she's heading out for the night. All you know is you're fighting again, and it's draining your soul. The next time it happens, remember these three things:

1. **It's okay to feel angry.** And it's okay for your cat to feel angry too. Many families are scared of anger, scared of what it might do. So they bottle it up, push it away, until it comes tumbling back out in even more counterproductive, hurtful ways. If your cat has upset you, you can tell him. And if he has something to say to *you*, buddy, you better sit down and listen and *take it in*. Don't let pride and your own insecurities do a number on your

cat. You're a man. A grown man who knows who he is and what his place is in the world. You can handle whatever that cat wants to throw at you. He may say hateful things. He may tell you that he never loved you and that you're not his real father. You will be okay. You will listen and accept and love.

2. **Identify your triggers.** What sets you off? When she stares at you with murder in her eyes? When he meows at your neighbor's door to be let into someone else's home? And how do those things make you feel? Threatened? Abandoned? Hurt? By recognizing your triggers *before* they're triggered, you can help control your anger and avoid an unpleasant meltdown.

3. **Give yourself a time-out.** When you feel yourself about to explode, remove yourself from the room and take a little you-time. What good will blowing up in your cat's face do? Count to ten, breathe deeply, and then reengage with your cat. And if you find your cat unwilling to take it down a notch, you can cut the fight short with an efficient "This is not a good conversation to have right now. Let's pick this up when we're both feeling a little calmer."

HOW TO TELL IF YOUR CAT IS HOOKED ON DRUGS

Your cat may "belong" to you, but the choices he makes are his own. And sometimes those choices will have dangerous consequences. Did you know that 1 in every 1.5 cats will experiment with drugs at some point in their lives?[8] Are you ready to help your little guy if he becomes a statistic? Because before you can help him, you need to be able to recognize the warning signs.

---

8   Including catnip.

The D.A.R.E. program is one of the most successful antidrug initiatives in the history of our nation. It has saved countless teens from a life of drugs, alcohol, and despair. Unfortunately, your cat doesn't attend public school. You two haven't been able to build up a bond of trust with the help of local police officers. Your cat may be on drugs. These are some of the warning signs:

- She's withdrawn, depressed, tired, and careless about personal grooming.
- He's hostile and uncooperative; he frequently knocks the lamp over.
- He's hanging around with a new group of friends.
- He's hanging around with a new group of drug addicts.
- Her grades have slipped, and her school attendance is irregular.
- He's lost interest in hobbies, sports, and other favorite activities.
- Her eating or sleeping patterns have changed; she's up at night and sleeps during the day.
- He has a hard time concentrating.
- He is checking in on Foursquare at known drug "hangout" spots.
- He has either gained or lost substantial weight.
- He has been listening to Pink Floyd with his bedroom door closed.
- He has sewn rock band patches onto his ripped denim jacket.
- She only wants a bunch of those "magic eye" posters for Christmas.
- Her eyes are red rimmed and/or her nose is runny in the absence of a cold.
- Household money has been disappearing.

A little catnip from time to time isn't a big deal, but once your cat or teenage child gets into the harder stuff, things can go very wrong very fast. Stay alert, and keep the lines of communication open. Remember: it's cool to care.

HOW TO TELL IF YOUR CAT OR
TEENAGE CHILD HAS JOINED A GANG

We try to watch out for our cats as much as we can, but sometimes even the best of cats falls in with the wrong crowd. Here are some telltale signs to watch out for:

- Is your cat wearing certain clothes or a certain color of clothes all the time?
- Is your cat's favorite movie *The Warriors*?
- Is your cat speaking in slang or cursing?
- Has your cat started acquiring body piercings and/or tattoos? Are they vulgar?
- Have your cat's grades in school declined?
- Is your cat sneaking out at night?
- Has your cat been tweeting about a "rumble"?

- Does your cat hear a recording of the West Coast Rap All-Stars' 1990 hit "We're All in the Same Gang" and sneer, "That's some corn-dog shit right there"?
- Did your cat ask for a switchblade for Hanukkah?
- Is your cat suddenly dropping "bling" like it's nobody's "biznass"?

If you answered yes to any of the preceding questions, your cat or teenage child may be in a gang. If this is the case, you may want to contact your local law enforcement and ask for counseling services.

REBUILDING THE TRUST

These kinds of crises can tear a family apart. The damage is not just to your cat; it strikes at the heart of your relationship with your cat—a relationship built on trust. Inspired by the D.A.R.E. program, I would like to offer you and your cat the opportunity to enter into a very special agreement: an agreement of mutual respect, trust, and love. If you and your cat are ready to take on these challenges, read and sign the agreement at right. You should cut it out of the book along the dotted lines, frame it, and put it in a place of prominence in your home.

Contract of Love

I recognize that there are many difficult decisions I face every day—like where to take my nap, which bag to hide in, when to stretch, what furniture to scratch, and what object of yours to knock over—and I commit to you that I will do everything in my power to avoid making decisions that will jeopardize my health, my safety and overall well-being, or your trust in me. I understand the dangers associated with these destructive behaviors and by signing below, I pledge my best-effort promise that I will do everything in my power to make a serious effort not to do them anymore (even though I'm a cat and so that sort of means that all bets are off).

_____   _____
CAT   **DATE**

I am committed to you and to your health and your safety and letting you sleep in my sock drawer. By signing below, I pledge to do everything in my power to communicate with you about the many difficult decisions you face. For instance, I will show you exactly which objects in my room are breakable and shouldn't be touched. I will also point out to you certain fabrics that are easily damaged if you scratch them. Also, I will show you pictures of certain friends and family members who are allergic to you and ask that you not sit in their lap or climb on them when they come over.

_____   _____
GUY   **DATE**

ABOUT RIGHT

CHAPTER 26

Responsible Cat Hoarding

If you're good at something, you should do it as much as possible. That makes sense, right? The truly successful in our world find their talent and commit their lives to it (just look at race car drivers, teachers, bridge builders, etc.). So if you are such a kickass cat owner, why on earth are you squandering your talents on just one cat?

HOW MANY CATS SHOULD I OWN?

Tough question, because owning multiple cats is a slippery slope. Two cats is twice as many as one cat, but three cats is only one more than two. Once you get to five or six, you won't even notice the difference in the quality of your life and state of your home. Try not to get bogged down in the math and go with your gut. Without meeting you personally, I'd recommend you own no more than fifteen cats.

Before bringing any new cats into the home, it's vital that you discuss these impending changes with your original (primary) cat. He may have some reservations. Listen to his concerns, and assure him that no matter how many dozens of cats end up living with you guys, you two will always have the tightest bond. He is your first and only true love, and no amount of additional cats will ever change that until he dies.

CAT HOARDING: THE BASICS

The key to building your horde is *slow but steady growth*. You only want to add one cat at a time, and you must allow the new group to become acclimated before adding another. I would recommend adding one cat a month. This schedule will keep you from topping out at fifteen cats for over a year. This will give you the time to keep up with any adjustments to food, water, and your own personal schedule you may need to make to take care of your new family.

After ten cats you will most likely need to quit your job to focus full-time on the horde. But really, did those people ever understand you? Did they cuddle with you? Did they sleep on your lap? Good riddance.

You may find that certain areas of your house "get away" from you as you're growing your brood. There is only so much cleaning you can do. If you have enough space to work with, I'd recommend simply sealing off rooms that have fallen into disarray or become filled with cat feces.

You've got a bushel of cats and you couldn't be happier. Your house literally mews and whines and sheds with life. You've got more than enough coming in from your unemployment insurance to feed almost all of the cats. But there's a difference between feeding their mouths and feeding their souls. How do you make sure they're all equally loved?

DON'T PLAY FAVORITES

There's no sense in breeding competition. All your cats are equally cute! Even if one is *extraordinarily* cute, you are still obligated as a parent of multiple cats to consider each "special in its own way." (It's okay to play favorites with your original cat, but never do that in front of the others. Save that for a stolen moment by the litter box room.)

DIVIDE UP YOUR TIME EQUALLY

If you pet one cat for five minutes and scratch his belly, you better be prepared to pet the other cat for five minutes and scratch her belly. You may find your petting of one cat interrupted by another cat inserting his body between your hand and the cat you thought you were petting, who is now wail-meowing some seriously heart-wrenching wail-meows. Well, you have two hands, don't you? Of course, if you have three or more cats to please, things can get tricky. You can *try* petting some of the cats with your feet, but unless you grew up playing soccer, it's doubtful you'll have the dexterity to satisfy them. Some cats may just have to wait their turn. Unfortunately, cats do not know the meaning of "wait your turn." If the natives are growing restless, try locking the extra cats in the closet for a while so you can focus on the two before you. Once they are satisfied, you can put *them* in the closet, remove two more, and work your way down the line. (Make sure not to forget about any cats you lock in the closet.)

More cats means more cat poop. It's just simple math. Each cat's digestive system is on its own clock, so to speak, so there's no telling how many times throughout the day you'll find a kitty dookie in the sandbox. Nothing says "that guy has way too many cats" like a collection of overripe kitty dookie, so make it a practice to scoop it as you see it. If you find that you're "seeing it" a little too often for your taste, you may want to avoid the litter box room for a stretch of days. I mean, how much cleaning is one man expected to do?

IS YOUR LARGE FAMILY OF CATS DOING GOD'S WORK?

Quite possibly! Who are we to judge?

DID YOU KNOW . . . ?

- Cats have no collarbone, so they can fit through any opening the size of their heads.
- Cats can jump up to five times their own height.
- Cats make approximately one hundred unique sounds, while dogs make ten.
- Male cats are called "toms"; female cats are called "queens" or "mollies."
- A group of adult cats is called a "clowder"; a group of kittens is called a "kindle."

- Spruce up your bachelor pad with your cat's best interests in mind—go pimp style for a cutting-edge street vibe, embrace feng shui for a New Agey rhythm, or just throw away all your possessions and leave nothing but you, your cat, and the bond you share.

- You can take your cat with you anywhere, even if you decide to stay right where you are.

- It's very easy to tell if your cat has been rubbing itself on someone else's leg.

- If you are worried that you're spending too much time with your cat, think it through. You're probably not spending *enough* time with your cat.

- Don't be scared of conflict with your cat. "Anger" may be only one letter away from "danger," but it's also only one letter away from "manger," and there's nothing scary about that.

- Watch out for early warning signs to keep your cat out of drugs, gangs, and other trouble.

Pop Quiz: *Which one of the following plants is* not *poisonous to cats?*

Aloe vera	Giant dumb cane
Amaryllis	Hahn's self-branching ivy
Cactus	Heartleaf philodendron
Calla lily	Indian rubber plant
Charming dieffenbachia	Lily
Chinese evergreen	Mistletoe
Chrysanthemum	Mother-in-law's tongue
Daffodil	Peace lily
Delphinium	Philodendron
Devil's ivy	Plumosa fern
Dicentra	Poinsettia
Dieffenbachia dumb cane	Rhododendron
Easter lily	Rubber plant
Elephant ears	Saddle leaf philodendron
English ivy	Satin pothos
Eucalyptus	Spotted dumb cane
Ferns	Sweetheart Ivy
Geranium	Tropic Snow Dieffenbachia
German ivy	

The answer is: None! All those plants are poisonous for cats!

FAMOUS CATS IN HISTORY

- CC, the first cloned cat
- Creme Puff, oldest cat, lived thirty-eight years
- Fred the Undercover Kitty, assisted NYPD in 2006
- Keyboard Cat,Internet phenomenon
- Maru, Internet celebrity, loves boxes
- Shiro, Internet celebrity, balances things on head
- Orangey, star of *Breakfast at Tiffany's*
- Trim, first cat to circumnavigate Australia
- Stubbs, elected mayor of Talkeetna, Alaska, in 1997 as write-in candidate
- Thelonius Monk, jazz musician, composer, and very cool cat

FAMOUS CAT LADY GUYS IN HISTORY

- Ernest Hemingway
- John Lennon
- Gustav Klimt
- Giorgio Armani
- Mark Twain
- Truman Capote
- Jean-Michel Basquiat
- Hunter S. Thompson
- Pope Benedict XVI
- Sir Winston Churchill
- Charles Dickens
- T. S. Eliot
- Albert Einstein
- Robert E. Lee
- Vladimir Lenin
- Muhammad
- Charles Lindbergh
- Sir Isaac Newton
- Nostradamus

**BAR GRAPH: COST OF CAT FOOD VS.
COST OF HANGING OUT AT A BAR**

HANGING OUT AT A BAR

CAT FOOD

PIE CHART: HOW TO DIVIDE UP YOUR DAY

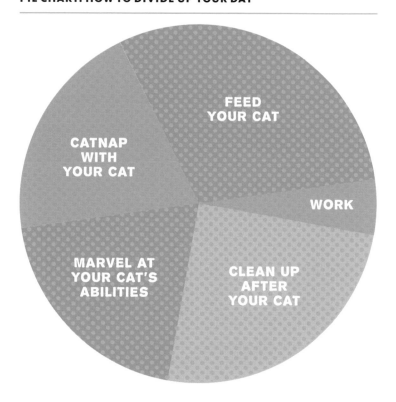

FEED
YOUR CAT

CATNAP
WITH
YOUR CAT

WORK

MARVEL AT
YOUR CAT'S
ABILITIES

CLEAN UP
AFTER
YOUR CAT

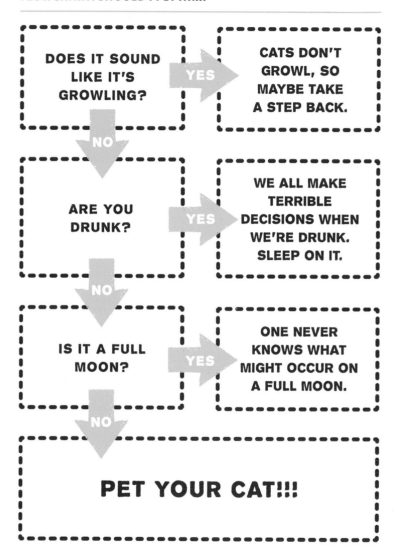

DOES IT SOUND LIKE IT'S GROWLING?

YES → **CATS DON'T GROWL, SO MAYBE TAKE A STEP BACK.**

NO ↓

ARE YOU DRUNK?

YES → **WE ALL MAKE TERRIBLE DECISIONS WHEN WE'RE DRUNK. SLEEP ON IT.**

NO ↓

IS IT A FULL MOON?

YES → **ONE NEVER KNOWS WHAT MIGHT OCCUR ON A FULL MOON.**

NO ↓

PET YOUR CAT!!!

CAT LADY PROGRESS REPORT #3:
HOW WELL DO YOU KNOW YOUR CAT?

The only way to know for sure is to play *The New Cat Game.*

Call your local bookseller and relay your book's ISBN number to the nice young man over the phone. You will soon receive a call from Bob Eubanks, longtime host of ABC's *The Newlywed Game.* He will invite you to sunny Burbank, California, for a taping of his new show, *The New Cat Game,* in which you will be asked a series of questions that only your cat knows the correct answers to.

Good luck, and safe travels!

FINAL EXAM

Are You a Cat Lady Yet?

True or False:

You don't own your cat; your cat owns you. _____

If you answered "true":

On a scale of 1 to 10 how much did you knowingly nod your head and/or follow up with "ain't that the truth"?

1 |——+——+——+——+——+——+——+——| 10

How many cats are currently in your home?

a. One. We live fairly independent lives from each other.

b. One. He/she is my best friend.

c. Two, three, four—the more the merrier! (Or should I say, the *meow* the merrier!)

d. I've lost count, but the sheriff says he counted more than thirty last week when he came by to check on me.

A few strays have started camping out in your backyard. You . . .

a. Scat them away! This isn't a feline halfway house.

b. Feed them, but never touch them. Who knows where they've been.

c. Feed them, name them, but maintain boundaries between your cats and the stranger cats, if only to guard against your own tendency toward attachment.

d. Feed them, name them, spay and neuter them, read aloud to them on cool nights.

How many of your cats are named after literary characters?

a. I only have one cat, and his name is Bob. So take that as you will.

b. I only have one cat and his name is Mr. Darcy Gigglesworth.

c. Do authors count as characters? I suppose *that's* up for discussion . . . [wink]!

d. I only read historical nonfiction. So . . . Trotsky, Truman, Robespierre, and Chief Seattle.

Please place the following items in your possession in quantity order from least to greatest:

○ Old magazines

○ Turner Classic Movies DVDs narrated by Robert Osborne

○ Saved birthday cards

○ Empty water bottles

○ Kitty litter boxes (please specify: industrial size?)

○ String, assorted

○ Cardboard boxes, purchased

○ Cardboard boxes, acquired

ANSWER SHEET

If you scored at least 4 out of 5 . . .

. . . then you, my friend, are a CAT LADY!

Congratulations! You have now officially completed your certification in Cat, which scientifically renders you both an Expert in Cat *and a* FULL. FLEDGED. CAT LADY!!!

Find your cat and give her a hug! You couldn't have done this without her!

The final steps are simple:

Tear out the attached certificate, and paste a picture of yourself where indicated.

Frame said certificate and hang it on your wall.

Love your cat(s) forever.

Official Cat Lady Guy Certification

**YOUR NAME AND
PHOTOGRAPH HERE**

Having completed the necessary courses required by this book is hereby declared a **CAT LADY GUY** and is therefore awarded this

DIPLOMA

with all the honors and privileges pertaining hitherto and thereof and in testimony wherein and herein and evermore been granted unto thee from here in perpetuity to the beneficence of what has heretofore been affixed.

CAT
GUY

Michael Showalter

Michael Showalter

Dawn Fleckner

Dawn Fleckner

State Comptroller of Cat Guy Certificates

_____

Your Signature

Cat Lady Guy
Hall of Fame

"iPod DJs are so lame. Me
and my kitty kick it old
school."

"Who's this pantsless weirdo
in the top hat? I want something to eat."

"Hey I'm a Cat Guy but I'm
also really sensitive and good
looking. Wanna fight?"

"My cat helps me write my
term papers. What does
yours do?"

"What you looking at buddy?! That's my gurl!"

"A man and his cat."

"Please, sit down. Let's chat. The three of us."

"Make him stop! I'm hungry and wanting to take a nap!"

"I knew these beer funnels would come in handy!"

"Hahahhahahahhaha- haaaaahhahhahaaahhaha!"

"That's not chest hair. That's a kitten."

"My cat just got a high score on being fat and lazy!"

"I love looking at my kitty."

"Me and my cat are a comedy duo."

"I'm so cool that even my cat seems really cool."

"Get off my back, Miss Jackson!"

"I coulda been somebody!
 I coulda been a contendah!"

"The journey is the reward."

"A board-certified Cat
 Lady Guy."

"Whassup with your hoodie?"

"Look ma! I caught a bear!"

"I don't go anywhere without
 my headphones or my cat!"

Thank you to Rebecca Kaplan, my editor, whose vision, enthusiasm, and humor have been a guiding force throughout this entire process. Thank you, Rebecca.

Thank you also to John Gall, Liam Flanagan, Deborah Aaronson, Steve Tager, Claire Bamundo, and everyone at ABRAMS, who have been so creative and wonderful to work with.

A huge, colossal, words-are-not-enough thank you to Stephie Grob-Plante whose contributions are evident on every single page of this book, from her hilarious and funny ideas to her amazing group of devoted friends who all agreed to spend a day with us shooting silly cat guy photos. I truly could not have done this without all of Stephie's inspiration and hard work. Thank you, Stephie. I also want to thank Krister Johnson, a friend, a brilliant and funny man (and fellow cat lady guy) who contributed so many great pieces of silliness to this book. Thank you, Krister.

I want to thank Son of Alan for his inspired and iconic artwork, Alison Grasso for her amazing photographs, and Kaela Wohl for her wonderfully archetypal costumes. I also want to acknowledge all of the people that helped out with our photo shoot: Tony Hernandez, John Skidmore, Matt Patches, Nina Hellman, Zack Akers, Bethany Reis, Dustin Pownall, Dave Yim, Steve Marcarelli, Andy Kabel, Ryan Fogarty, George Robert Morse, Daniel Lugo, Josh Terrill, Russ Frushtick, Chris Littler, Courtney Littler, Chris Plante, Kara Donaldson, Katie Akana, and Anne Kilcullen.

I also want to thank all of the cat lady guys out there in the world wide web who so graciously donated intimate and revealing photos of themselves lovin' on their kitties.

I would also like to thank my manager, Peter Principato, my lawyer, Rick Genow, and everyone at UTA. Plus a special thank-you to Ben Greenberg for introducing me to Rebecca Kaplan and ABRAMS and also for being my good pal, collaborator, and confidant.

Thank you to my mom and dad, Elaine and English, for always encouraging me to pursue my silly ambitions ("Hey Mike, you should write a cat book!") and thanks to the Lafleurs and the Ellis crew for your constant support and good humor.

Finally, thank you to my wife, Kalin: my fellow cat lover, my best friend, and the first person who sees anything I do. If she laughs, I know I'm pointed in the right direction.

Finally, finally, thank you to Louie, Billy, Tim, and Sally. My cats. Even though you mostly just take naps and knock things over, you are a constant source of amazement to me. Meow!

EDITOR: Rebecca Kaplan
DESIGNER: Liam Flanagan
PRODUCTION MANAGER: Anet Sirna-Bruder

Library of Congress Control Number: 2013936013

ISBN: 978-1-4197-0690-5

Abrams Image books are available at special discounts when purchased
in quantity for premiums and promotions as well as fundraising or
educational use. Special editions can also be created to specification. For
details, contact specialsales@abramsbooks.com or the address below.

ABRAMS The Art of Books
115 West 18th Street, New York, NY 10011
abramsbooks.com